T0166060

HAUNTING IN BIG BEAR LAKE

HAUNTING IN BIG BEAR LAKE

A True Story

JODI POLOS

Copyright © 2011 by Jodi Polos.

Library of Congress Control Number: 2011917080
ISBN: Hardcover   978-1-4653-6988-8
               Softcover   978-1-4653-6987-1
               Ebook   978-1-4653-6989-5

All rights reserved. No part of this book may be reproduced or transmitted in any form or by any means, electronic or mechanical, including photocopying, recording, or by any information storage and retrieval system, without permission in writing from the copyright owner.

This book is a work of non-fiction. Names and places have been changed to protect the privacy of all individuals. The events and situations are true.

This book was printed in the United States of America.

To order additional copies of this book, contact:
Xlibris Corporation
1-888-795-4274
www.Xlibris.com
Orders@Xlibris.com

This book is dedicated to Jami, my identical twin sister, who I love so much. To my husband, Phillip, the love of my life, I could never have made it through life without you by my side. To my daughters for giving me so much love and encouragement through the difficult times that I had to endure.

ACKNOWLEDGMENTS

I have so many people that I would like to thank for assisting me in writing this book. First and most importantly is my husband, Phillip. I have been blessed to have been with you since I met you in Jami's class at fifteen years of age. I am so glad we changed that class. I love you so much.

My daughter Brittney for doing the Creative Editing of this book. Thank you for helping me. I am so proud of you. I love you so much.

My daughter Katie, Thank you for also helping me with this book. I am so proud of you. You're a wonderful daughter and sister. I love you so much too.

Brea, Sara, and Grace—I love you all so much and I am truly blessed to have such wonderful daughters.

Tom, thank you for all of your help throughout the writing of this book. The most wonderful part of this experience was seeing you again after over twenty years. I will always think of you as my big brother who always looked out for Jami and me. Thank you for believing in us and protecting us throughout our childhood.

Karen, you have been such a wonderful true friend since elementary school. Writing this book gave me the chance to visit with you after so many years had passed. Jami and I were so fortunate to have you as our friend. Thank you for listening to us when we were scared and believing us. Many hugs and love, my dear friend.

Ronda, you were the very best friend we could have hoped for. There were so many fun times. When things were scary or tough, you always made the situation better with your brilliant humor and megawatt smile. Jami and I loved and appreciated your friendship so much. I value your friendship just as much now as I did then. Love you, my friend.

Margaret and the Stratton family, you have been a kind and lifelong friend. What your dad did for me by playing the bagpipes for Jami was the most beautiful thing I have ever witnessed. We have been friends since elementary school, and Jami and I were blessed to have you in our lives as children, and as adults.Much love and hugs to you and your family.

Bill Bennett, Thank you for all of your guidance and support.Iam truly blessed to have you in my life.

INTRODUCTION

My name is Jodi. I was born on June 29, 1970, along with my identical twin Jami. We were born a month early, and my parents had no idea that they were having twins. Jami was the physically larger, stronger twin, and she weighed over six pounds. I was the fragile three-pound twin and my lungs had not developed completely. Jami was able to go home with our mother a few days after our birth. Unfortunately, I was so small and premature that I couldn't go home for a month, until I had become strong enough to leave the hospital.

Both Jami and I had light brown hair and hazel eyes with light complexions; the only difference was our weights at birth.

Jami and I were very close and attached to one another from birth. We shared a crib and always wanted to be together; we even shared bedrooms throughout our childhood when we didn't have to. Being a twin is like you have another half of you, and you don't feel right or complete unless you're with your twin. That was what it was like for Jami and me. Many of our relatives told us stories about how we interacted when we were little. Jami and I would communicate in a language that only the two of us understood. My brother also told us that on many occasions he observed the two of us just staring at each other and nodding our heads as if saying yes or no, but we would not be talking. It seemed as if Jami and I would read each other's thoughts and communicate. Being a twin has been such a wonderful experience.

Jami and I had a dream home life when we were little. We had our mother, father, and our two big brothers. Our brothers were so sweet and treated Jami and I like little princesses. Jami and I had a different father from that of our brothers. We all lived at that time with our mother and father. Our mother had sole custody of my brothers, and they were being raised by our father.

Jami and I were four years old and living in Las Vegas when our entire world changed. My mother needed a hysterectomy right away because of some underlying medical condition. My mother had the surgery, and it would be five weeks before she would recover. The fifth week finally came; so she went for her post-op checkup. The Doctor told her that she was fit to resume her regular movement and lifting.

My mother had been housebound for the last five weeks and wanted to go out to dinner with her friends and visit them. I was told that at some point during the dinner our mother started to have severe pain in her leg and wanted to go home. When our mother came home, she told our father she wasn't feeling good. She was on the bed lying down when my father checked on her and she was cold and dead. It turned out that our mother died because of a blood clot. She was not fit to resume her daily activities, and the Doctor had made the wrong recommendation.

Immediately our brothers whom we loved so much were sent far away to their abusive father, and we hardly saw them again. Jami and I were sent away to our uncle. Our father was not given an option to raise us. Our uncle also lived in Las Vegas at that time. When our mother died, he wanted a fresh change for all of us, and he took a job that was offered to him in Big Bear. Soon after our mother's death, we packed up all of our belongings and moved to Big Bear Lake with our uncle.

Throughout the years as Jami and I grew up, I had turned into the more protective twin. I felt as if I was the big sister who had to watch out for Jami. Jami really needed me to look out for her from childhood to adulthood. For whatever reason, I was the more level-headed twin who made better decisions.

We lived most of our childhood in Big Bear Lake, California, and Las Vegas, Nevada. We moved back and forth a few times between both states and lived in many different houses. I had never lived in a house like the one Jami and I were about to move into.

There were houses with really scary histories to the home, and then there were the houses that no one really knew anything about. With most houses, only the builder knew what had been there on the land before the home was built or the history of the area.

The new house that we were about to move into no one knew anything about the previous tenants. The few things that I knew about Big Bear before it became populated were some few bits. Big Bear was a hunting area for a Native American tribe before the Gold Rush hit. When the Gold Rush occurred, Gold Miners started trickling in from all over the country, hoping to strike it rich. The area where this story occurred eventually became a cattle ranch. The cattle ranch property later was sold off to then become individual homes.

The houses that Jami and I had lived in throughout the years were all comfortable and not scary in the least bit. No one will ever know what makes a house haunted or terrifying to live in. I can tell you I have lived in a house that was an exception to what people imagine a haunted house to be. This story is a true account of the occurrences that happened in the Big Bear Lake house. The only things that I have changed are some names and genders of specific people in this true story to protect their privacy.

1 | MOVING INTO THE NEW HOUSE

THE YEAR WAS 1984, AND Jami and I were fourteen years old and just about to turn fifteen. This is a true account of what I and others witnessed during that time in Big Bear Lake. We were told that our family was moving into a new large two-story home. The day had come to move into the house tucked way up in the mountain.

Our new house was located in an area of Big Bear Lake, which was called the *Moonridge* area. We turned onto the street where the new house stood. My uncle started to slow down, and there it was the perfect home. Jami and I started saying, "This house is the best house that we have ever lived in." Unfortunately, our uncle told us that the pretty house was not ours; it was the house next to that one. We pulled into the driveway, and there it was the new house.

Jami and I were obviously not expecting to see what was right before us. We had envisioned such a pretty home in the mountains, and that house was nothing like what we had thought. The house was dark and rustic. The wood on the house was worn out and in need of painting. There were old-fashioned stained glass windows with the main color being red. The house had a wooden deck that led to the upstairs entry door. The outside stairs appeared to be old and rickety as we walked over to the steps before entering through the downstairs entry door. As I stood on the stairs, I noticed that the wooden handrail that had once been smooth wood was now nothing but worn out wood with chipped paint. As I looked at the handrail, I knew that Jami and I were going to get a lot of splinters from the old painted wood.

There were a few different entries to get into the house. There was a front entry door for the downstairs, directly below the upstairs front door. The driveway pulled right up to the downstairs entry door. That was really convenient for us. Many of the houses in the area had a lot of stairs that you would have to hike up just to get to the front door. The winter would turn the stairs into sheets of ice, and you could get hurt very easily from slipping on the outside steps.

Jami and I observed the outside of the house, and it was really creepy. There was no grass or plants outside, just one medium-sized pine tree that didn't look healthy, surrounded by a mound of dirt. That was how the front yard looked. The house was so dark and dreary from the outside that I hoped the inside of the house would make up for the dark, ominous appearance of the outside.

Our uncle took out his keys, opened the door, and said that the entire downstairs area was his and the upstairs area was for Jami and me.

We all entered the house through the front door downstairs. We ran through his room where there was a thick bright blue shag carpet. I had never seen a carpet like that before. That was the brightest part of the house. The shag carpet felt like tall soft grass under our feet. The walls downstairs were all made of dark wood paneling. In the middle of the room against the wall was an antique cast iron potbelly wood burning stove. I had only seen something like that in the old Western movies. We ran through our uncle's room to the door that led to the staircase so we could go upstairs.

I opened the door to the stairs and straight ahead was another door. We were curious about what was behind that door. We thought that it was probably a small closet. Jami and I looked ahead of us at that long dark staircase that went upstairs. The stairs were made of wood and had no carpet. The stairwell was really steep and dark. At the top of the stairs near the top there was a square area that then went toward the left, leading to the upstairs area. That square area at the top of the stairs will be a very important part in my story.

Jami and I stared at that oddly placed room at the bottom of the stairs, then Jami opened the door. I looked over Jami's shoulder as she flipped on the light switch, and we saw a dark room that was not finished. The room was built into the hillside of the house, and the floor was made of packed dry mud. The roof and two of the walls were the only cemented portion in that room. The other walls were of packed dry mud and so was most of the floor. Certain areas of the Mud Room were damp, and the room had an old, musty smell to it. The room was cold, dark, and damp. Jami and I didn't like that room; something just wasn't right about it. Being in that room just felt like being in a hidden chamber against your will. The feeling was very odd and we didn't like that room. So we quickly closed the door, not wanting to even be in there. Later on, the Mud Room would lead us to find something which in turn could lead to an entirely new story and investigation.

I closed the door, and it was time to run up the staircase. Jami and I looked for a light switch, but there wasn't one. The only light for the staircase was from the sunlight upstairs that gave you just enough lighting to make out the stairs. The staircase was dark and dangerous with no proper lighting. As we walked up the steep stairs, you could hear the creaking in the wood below our feet.

To this day, I remember the feeling that I had as I climbed the steps. There was a very intense feeling; it was like I was being watched by something that could not be seen. There was also a claustrophobic feeling that made me want to get up the stairs as fast as possible. Jami and I had never experienced those odd feelings before. Later as the months passed, our feelings reached the point where we would never go up or down that staircase unless we were with each other or had our dogs with us.

My dog was around five years old and her name was Frenchy; she was an ivory white-colored Maltese and poodle mix. She was my fearless little best friend who hardly left my side. Jami's dog was Frenchy's mother and she was around ten years old. Jami's dog was named Missy. Missy was an apricot-colored poodle mix. Missy was always by Jami's side as Frenchy was always by mine. As time went on, I found out why the stairs were so terrifying to us.

We were excited to see the upstairs area. The entire upstairs area was going to be ours. The upper floor had a huge red brick fireplace in the living room and next to that was the kitchen. After the kitchen, there was a bathroom and two bedrooms with a hallway that ran down the middle. The walls were all the same, like downstairs that had dark wood paneling. The floor was a dark-colored hardwood that matched the walls.

Jami and I had a choice of whichever bedroom we wanted, and we decided on the bedroom that had a set of antique wooden bunk beds. The bunk beds were left behind by the previous owners. Jami and I were excited about our new room because we had never had bunk beds before. I took the top bunk and Jami had the bottom. Jami and I had always shared a room, and now there was so much more space without two beds taking up an entire room.

The upstairs area had a lot of antiques throughout, which were left behind by the earlier owners. There were numerous kerosene lamps that were used a lot. Most of the kerosene lamps were almost empty and the wicks had been burned on being used so much. There was an antique velvet floral couch, which was the ugliest couch we had ever seen. There were side tables and end tables with antique lamps on them. Looking throughout the house, it was almost like looking back in time, seeing so many antiques. We had never seen antiques before for real. The television was the only place where we had ever seen pieces like those before. What surprised me was that those antiques were valuable items. Why would anyone leave them behind and take everything else? It didn't make sense.

When the day came to move our belongings into the new house, our friend of many years, Tom, came up from Las Vegas to help out. Tom was a friend whom Jami and I had met when we lived in Las Vegas many years before. Jami and I had been seven then and Tom seventeen. Tom lived five houses up from our home. There was this amazing dog named Max, who was a German Shepherd. Max belonged to Tom's family. Max would constantly jump over Tom's fence and run down to our house and play with us. Tom, then, constantly had to walk down to our house to take *Max* back home. Over time, we developed a friendship of a lifetime with Tom because he was constantly at our house picking up Max.

Tom had blond curly hair and hazel eyes; he was a senior in high school and on the football team at that time. He had come to our house so many times to get Max that he became like family to our uncle, Jami, and I. He became the big brother that we had longed for since our big brothers had been taken away from us. Tom had a great sense of humor and that great laugh. He fit right into our family. When Tom was around, life was brighter and more fun.

Tom had come from Las Vegas to visit and help us move into the new house. Tom ended up spending the majority of his summer with us and many weekends too, then eventually moved to Big Bear for a few years. Tom was now in his early twenties and more grown up. Tom had aged a few years, but he was still young at heart and never lost his sense of humor.

When Tom would visit, he would sleep in the bedroom across from ours. Jami and I always felt safe when Tom was in the room across from ours. We spent many days and nights playing board games and card games with Tom and listening to the stereo as loud as we wanted. The fun times slowly deteriorated because of unexplainable events that started occurring on a regular basis in the house. As time passed, Tom became the main target of many physical attacks. Soon Tom developed the same uneasy fears that Jami and I had.

The house had a high pitched ceiling .When I looked up in the corners of the ceiling there were cobwebs and spiders all over .It was creepy having so many spiderwebs thru out the upstairs .Most of these spiderwebs were unreachable. So we had no choice but to live with spiders above us in certain areas of the house. The house was over run with what we called Daddy Long Leg Spiders. This kind of spider had a small body and super long legs. It was the scariest feeling when one of those spiders would come down from the ceiling and land on you. The spiders would always show up on someone when they were not expecting it. On a regular basis we would jump up screaming and frantically brush the spiders off of us. Tom was not bothered to much by the spiders ,but Jami and I sure were.

The scary occurrences were mild at first. When I say mild, I mean things began happening, like hearing footsteps on the creaking wooden floor and stairs. When no one was in the room with you, things would fall off the shelves. There was really no way to explain the atmosphere in the house. It felt as though something was watching every move we made, and it was scary.

Jami and I were just teenagers, and we didn't feel comfortable living in that house. We had nowhere else to live, and we were stuck living in that creepy house. My uncle was a very busy man and completely oblivious to the paranormal phenomena going on. He wouldn't believe anything that Jami, Tom, or I ever told him when it came to the strange and scary occurrences going on.

Our relationship with our uncle wasn't a very good one. He had his own busy life, and it seemed that Jami and I were a burden on him. Our uncle may have raised us, but he didn't listen to our concerns or worries. I honestly don't believe he even loved us and that if he could have given us up he would have in a heartbeat. A guilty conscience is the only reason I think he had us. The stress between our uncle and us was tense. The only nice thing about the house was that he stayed downstairs most of the time when he was home, so we didn't have to see him too much.

Jami and I loved the idea of having the entire upstairs all to ourselves; it meant less stress from our uncle and for us too. Unfortunately, that feeling was short lived. Jami and I soon realized we were not alone upstairs, and the stress got worse than we could have ever imagined.

2 | ODD OCCURRENCES

THE FIRST SIGN THAT SOMETHING was not right occurred shortly after we moved into the house that summer. The heater was turned off because our uncle said we couldn't afford the high gas bills. He told us the only way to heat the house was to use the fireplace.

Next to the huge red brick fireplace there was this large metal key. The metal key was how you turned the gas on and off. Our uncle was showing Tom, Jami, and I how to use the gas fire starter. Our uncle turned on the key and then lit a match and dropped it into the starter's burners. Instantly, there was a large explosion, and a huge bright orange and red fireball blew our uncle across the room.

I hurried and turned the key off as Jami ran to his side to help him; he was dazed and scared. Our uncle had singed hairs on his arm and other areas of his face. He was very fortunate that he was not burned which would have been worse. That explosion could easily have killed him or the house would have caught fire. Our uncle told us that we were not allowed to use the fire starter again. So then when we had to start a fire, we would use crumpled up paper to start the fire. Starting a fire without the gas starter made it a lot harder and to heat the upstairs area.

The fireplace provided very little heat for the entire upstairs area. The fireplace was so inefficient. The heat could only be felt right up close to the fire. The two bedrooms had no heat, and it was always so cold in our room. Jami and I would wrap ourselves in several blankets and sleep on the ground by the fireplace on the coldest of nights. Tom would sleep on the couch so he would stay warm too. The upstairs always remained cold, no matter how long we had a roaring fire going. The heat just didn't affect the temperature of the upstairs. Jami and I would take turns all night long putting more logs in the fireplace to make sure the fire didn't go out. Lying on that cold wooden floor was so uncomfortable and hard to sleep on. No wonder we didn't get good grades in school; we were so tired from being up throughout the night as we were so cold.

There seemed to be no way to get the upstairs area warm. We were constantly cold in every room upstairs, but the downstairs was always warm. Now that I look back I've read that hauntings usually occurred in cold spots of homes. I didn't know that back then, but now I think that's why the upstairs area was constantly cold.

To combat the cold, we had to spend most of our summer cutting and stacking wood to prepare for the winter.

Wood cutting was very important but extremely strenuous work. We had to stock the entire area of the backyard with wood to be used as our only source of heat during the winter. Winters were very cold, and we would have a lot of snow that made our house feel like an igloo. We would bring home the trees that were marked to be cut down. Once we got the wood home, there would always be large pieces of wood that needed to be split into smaller usable pieces.

To split the large pieces of wood, we used a metal wedge along with a heavy wood-splitting metal mallet. The mallet was used like an ax. We would place the metal wedge onto the wood and start swinging the mallet into the wood till it split into a smaller usable piece.

Usually, Jami or I would have to hold the wedge during the wood splitting, but Tom was visiting, so he helped our uncle that day. Tom was holding the metal wedge while our uncle hit the wood with the heavy metal mallet. It took a great deal of faith to trust anyone to swing a heavy mallet toward your head. Tom had every bit of faith that our uncle could swing that heavy mallet and never miss his mark. Jami and I hated that part of wood cutting. I didn't trust anyone swinging that mallet so close to my head or hand.

Our uncle always said, "Don't worry. I've never missed before."

My feeling about that phrase was "He has not missed *yet!*"

They both had a long day ahead and began splitting the big pieces of wood. A few hours into wood cutting, our uncle was called in to work. Tom proceeded to split the wood by himself. Jami and I were inside the house when we heard Tom yelling from outside. Both of us ran outside to see what had happened. As we ran outside, we discovered that Tom was bleeding profusely from his shoulder.

Tom was perplexed because he had no idea what had just happened. Tom held his arm and said aloud that he thought he had been shot. That turned out to be a freak accident. When Tom swung the mallet, a large sliver of metal broke off the metal wedge. Then to make matters worse, somehow the sliver that broke off shattered into tiny metal shards of dangerously small sharp pieces. One of the tiny metal fragments had embedded itself into Tom's arm.

When Tom realized what had happened, he quickly got into the SUV and took himself to the Emergency Room. Tom was in the ER with the Doctor. We waited at home to hear from someone about Tom's condition. Finally, Tom called us at home to tell us about what had happened while he was in the hospital.

The Doctor had explained to Tom what needed to be done to fix his arm. The fragment that had broken off had actually gone deeper into Tom's arm more than anyone had thought. The metal fragment was in Tom's vein, traveling through his body, and was on its way to Tom's heart. The Doctor said that when the metal fragment reached Tom's heart he would die.

The Doctor needed to find out where the metal fragment was and pull that piece out before it killed Tom. The Doctor finally found the general location of the metal fragment. Tom had to be put through a painful surgery and yet be wide awake. The Doctor surgically cut open Tom's skin on both sides of his arm and kept them clamped back. The

Doctor urgently searched for the fragment in Tom's vein. The metal shard was quickly traveling to Tom's heart, and the Doctor had to be quick in finding and pulling out the metal shard.

The Doctor finally found the fragment and successfully removed it. The Doctor held up the little metal shard with his instrument and showed it to Tom and said, "This is just like the old days when they removed bullets." Tom looked at the shard as the Doctor held it up to show him what that fragment looked like. The Doctor then tossed the metal fragment into a metal can. Tom said it was just like an old Western movie. In a lot of Western movies, the Doctor would remove the bullet and toss it into a metal can, and you could hear that very distinct noise that the metal makes as the bullet drops into the metal can. Tom said the feeling of what had just happened reminded him and the Doctor of an old Western movie where there is the scene that someone is having a bullet removed.

The removal of the shard had been a success. The Doctor then stapled together the open skin; he went on to say that he had never seen a wedge split apart and hurt someone before. The Doctor went on to say that Tom was very lucky to have gotten to the hospital when he did. Tom wouldn't have had much time left before he would have died from that fragment reaching his artery.

Tom was very fortunate to have a hospital only five minutes away from our house. Most small mountain communities didn't have hospitals in the 1980s. If we had not had a hospital close by Tom would have died because of that injury. The closest hospital other than the Big Bear one was an hour away. I believe that that was the beginning of the supernatural attacks against Tom. My greatest worry was that something in that house was very real and dangerous. Whatever entity was in the house was capable of hurting all of us and we had no way to protect ourselves.

Jami and I had begun feeling scared and uneasy in that house. We decided to talk to Tom about what was going on in the house. We were grateful to have Tom to confide in. Tom was lying in his bed, recovering from his surgery, and we asked Tom if we could talk to him about the house. Jami and I asked Tom if he had felt that the house could be haunted. Tom said that yes, he did think the house was haunted. Tom believed in the possibility of paranormal activity.

Tom, having the same belief about the house that we had, actually made us feel confident that what was happening wasn't just our imagination. Tom went on to tell us about an experience that had horrified him years earlier. Tom began telling us about what he had witnessed.

Tom said, "It happened in the evening and it was dark outside." He had seen something outside his window from across his bedroom. Tom walked over to get a better look at what it was that he saw by his window. There was a tree that was next to his window, and to his horror, there was a black distorted-looking figure with red eyes staring at him through his window. Tom saw that thing with glowing red eyes looking into his room, standing right next to the windowsill. The figure was watching Tom. Then the figure in the tree just vanished. That story was scary enough for us to wish we had not just listened to it. We now knew that Tom had seen something supernatural and he believed in hauntings.

Tom had to take it easy for a bit and not move around too much while his shoulder healed. Later that night, Tom was in his bed and we were all going to sleep. To our surprise, Tom ran out of his bedroom and ran to the front door. Tom had the upstairs front door open, and he was looking outside. It turned out that Tom had run to see what had been looking at him through his window. Tom was wide awake and he had looked at the window, and there was this massive black thing that was so big it blocked most of the window. Tom thought that it must have been a bear. That happened a lot with Tom. On a regular basis, Tom would run out of his room to the outside trying to catch a glimpse of whatever that was outside his window. Keep in mind, he was supposed to be recovering and not moving around a lot. Finally, Tom realized that there was no bear. That was something else, and the thought that something that large was watching Tom was very scary. We never found out what the figure was outside his window.

Tom had no window coverings; that is why he was sure of what he was seeing outside his window. Jami and I did have window coverings, and we started to wonder if that thing was watching us through our window.

Our shades were made of thin white lace curtains. The curtains were very easy to see through into our bedroom from the outside. Jami and I got to the point that if we felt like we were being watched we wouldn't look toward the window. Neither Jami nor I wanted to see what Tom was seeing. Knowing that something was watching us through the windows from the outside was already scary enough, but then something was also watching us from inside the house.

3 | THE LIGHTS AND THE GHOST DOG

THE LIGHTS IN THE HOUSE were switched off at night except for one light in the hallway. Tom started to hear someone walking around, and he thought that maybe Jami or I were up. When Tom walked into the living room, he realized every light had been turned on in the house and Jami and I were both asleep, so it wasn't us. So Tom then proceeded to turn off all of the lights like they were meant to be.

The next night, Tom heard the noises of footsteps again. Tom ran out of his room to see who was up. As Tom entered the living room, he saw again that every light had been turned on upstairs. There was something that was turning on the lights, and there was no way to explain that.

The footsteps and turning on all of the lights went on for almost a month. Tom constantly tried to catch a glimpse of whatever was walking around the house at night, turning on all of the lights. Unfortunately, it was impossible to catch that phenomenon as it happened. Every time Tom raced out of his room, it was too late; the lights were all instantly turned on. The monthly electric bill came in, and my uncle was furious. Our uncle blamed Jami and me for the high electric bill. Tom tried explaining what had been happening, but he refused to believe Tom. Now whatever that was there had caused us to be reprimanded. We couldn't do anything to stop the lights from turning on every night by themselves. After we were yelled at by our uncle, the lights didn't turn on every night like they had been. The lights then were turned on sporadically.

In a way, things were now scarier. When we all thought that whatever was responsible for turning on every light upstairs had gone away, that was when the lights would all turn on. As for the footsteps at night, those never went away either. You never knew when you were going to hear the footsteps that belonged to no one. That entity in our house always caught all of us off guard with the lights being turned on and with creaking steps being heard. It was as if the entity knew when our guard was down, and that was when we would be taunted or a physical attack would occur.

Frenchy my dog had been named after the character Frenchy in the movie *Grease*. Frenchy was my absolute best friend, and she never left my side, that is never until we moved into that house.

Dogs are able to sense things that humans don't sense. That could explain Frenchy's behavior while we lived in that house. One day, I was upstairs sitting on the couch watching TV, and I saw Frenchy slowly coming up the stairs and begin walking toward me. I called to her and patted my lap for her to come to me, but she didn't come. Frenchy was acting very odd. I didn't understand why my dog refused to run and jump up into my lap as she always used to do. Frenchy appeared to be in a trance and didn't even know I was there. She had never ignored me before, but that time she ignored me and continued walking slowly past me as if I was not there.

I called Frenchy's name louder and louder, but she acted as if she couldn't hear me. She walked around the corner and down the hall and then entered the bathroom. I got up and walked down the hallway to see what she was doing. When I reached the bathroom door, I saw her walking behind the toilet. I called to her, but she ignored me and kept on walking. I walked over and got down on my hands and knees to pick up

Frenchy. When I reached behind the toilet where she had gone, she was not there. Frenchy had vanished in thin air.

There was no way my dog could have come back past me without me seeing her because I had watched her the entire time as she walked behind the toilet. As I stood up and turned around, there was Frenchy standing at the doorway to the bathroom. I looked at her and said, "Frenchy, how did you do that?" I called to her, but she was frightened and would not enter the bathroom.

I walked to the doorway and picked up Frenchy. I took her with me back into the living room and didn't think much about what had happened. I was not frightened at the time. I was mostly just perplexed at how she could have ended up behind me at the bathroom doorway when I didn't see her pass by.

A few days later, I was sitting on the couch again, and Frenchy came up the stairs and walked past me very slowly just like before. Frenchy was just two feet away from me, ignoring all my calls for her to come to me. I was becoming angry because she was ignoring me. I yelled out her name, but she continued on her way again into the bathroom. I followed Frenchy into the bathroom, and once again she went behind the toilet. I ran to catch her and looked behind the toilet, and she had disappeared again. One more time, Frenchy had vanished right before my eyes.

I turned around, and Frenchy was standing at the bathroom doorway again. This time she stood at the doorway and backed away, looking frightened. Frenchy whimpered, backed away, and then ran down the hallway. I stood there and got a cold chill that tingled down my spine, and I became very frightened that I was witnessing a whole new paranormal situation.

Frenchy had never been afraid of anything. She was a tough little dog and had always been fearless. I thought if there was something in the bathroom that was bad enough to scare her, I better get out of there myself. I began to realize that it may not have been my Frenchy but a ghost of Frenchy that I had followed into the bathroom both times only to see her vanish.

I ran downstairs to find Jami. I was really shaken and told Jami what had just happened. What I told Jami then scared her. The two of us took our dogs, Frenchy and Missy, and left the house until our uncle got home from work. Jami and I would do anything to keep out of the house until an adult came home.

1 | KEEPING BUSY

JAMI AND I CONSTRUCTED OUR own tree house close by our bedroom window. We used whatever wood we could find on our property or in the forest to build it. The tree house, the forest, and the lake became our place of safety and comfort. On the nights that we were terrorized, Jami and I would sneak out of our bedroom window and sleep in our tree house.

When it was summer, we would go walk down to the zoo and look at the animals through the fence and watch the horses graze in the pasture nearby. Sometimes we would be too scared to be in the house in the daytime too. One of the places that Jami and I would go to was the lake. We would ride our bikes down there and go fishing, or we would just bring a towel and lie in the sun by the lake. I am not sure when it happened, but Jami and I stopped going to the lake because of a huge outbreak of frogs. Jami and I were walking through the field toward the lake when all of a sudden all you could see were frogs all over. We couldn't take a step without squishing the little frogs. Then the frogs would all start jumping up and land on us. That was so creepy. There were so many frogs that they consumed an area of the main street near the Interlaken shopping center. That area had a lot of traffic, and there was no way for cars to avoid running over the frogs. Jami and I looked, and we stood in shock at all of those frogs that had just shown up out of nowhere and were migrating into the main street surely to their doom. The noise of the cars running over the frogs was gross. Then some of the frogs hopped onto the street and actually hopped right into cars' windshields and splat. I wonder if there were any accidents caused by the frogs. So then Jami and I lost one of our safe places to go. The lake was not an option to go to any longer. That seemed like something out of the Bible—the Plague of Frogs.

During the summer, we looked forward to going to the Movie Theater for the evening show and then hang out with our friends after watching the newest summer blockbuster movie. I don't know if there was any truth to this but almost every time we went to the movies with our friends, someone would say that it was haunted. When you talk to most locals, a lot of them will still agree with that theory. When we went to the movies or to the park, we usually hung out with Karen and Ronda.

Karen was always funny, spunky, and was almost always seen wearing her fedora hat. Karen avoided the big crazy 1980s, hair and had her own distinct look. Jami and I felt safe talking with Karen about the things going on in our house because she was so kind and not judgmental. Later as we got to know Karen, we heard of the stories of *The Knickerbocker* mansion being haunted. It turned out that Karen's last name was Knickerbocker. We never asked her about the rumors of her family's home. I figured that if she wanted to tell us anything she would when she was ready to.

The other thing that kept us busy was sleeping over at our friend Ronda's house. Ronda had fire engine red hair with lots of freckles. Ronda was always laughing or joking around. Nothing ever seemed scary when we were with her. Ronda also knew of the things going on in our house, and she felt bad for us whenever we had to go home. Ronda would live to see a horrible sight twenty years later with Jami, but you will have to read on to find out what she saw.

During the winter when we would sneak out of our room, we would spend our time sledding in the middle of the night. The only light we had when we would sled at night was the moonlight. That was actually pretty fun sledding down the street in the middle of the night. Jami and I became very creative at keeping ourselves busy when we were too scared to sleep in the house.

We always brought our dogs with us for protection. Looking back now, our little poodle and Maltese really didn't stand a chance, protecting us from being attacked by a wild animal. At that age, ignorance was bliss.

We actually felt safer outside in the middle of the night in the forest instead of sleeping in that house. No wonder Jami and I continued to have bad grades at that point. We stayed up almost all night every night and would be exhausted in the morning. We would always return home just before the sun came up. We never got caught by our uncle. The only people who knew we did that were some of our friends who would spend the night at our house.

Eventually, friends too didn't want to spend the night at our house anymore. They were too scared to stay at our house. All of our friends who had ever spent the night in that house all had the same experiences and feelings of fear when they slept over. All our close friends knew about what we were living through. The only times of relief that Jami and I got were when we started spending the night at friends' houses. It felt so good to go to sleep and not be scared of the noises, voices, and figures.

It was fall, and the trees were all changing colors. The orange leaves on the trees along with the multiple colors of the forest at that time of the year were breathtaking. During that time, we found out that my dog, Frenchy, was pregnant.

Frenchy soon gave birth to a litter of three puppies. All of them were pure white in color and they all looked exactly like Frenchy. The puppies were only a few days old, and it was already turning into a harsh, cold winter. During that time, our uncle planned a trip for us to go to Las Vegas to visit our cousins. We knew we would be gone for two days. We put our dogs in the bathroom with lots of food and water because we didn't know anyone whom we could ask to come and let them out and take care of them for us.

That was a big problem for me, and I had a grave concern for the newborn puppies because of the cold weather. Our uncle refused to let us keep the heater on for the dogs. The bathroom would be freezing cold inside just like the outside. I made a dog bed for them out of a cardboard box, and I put towels and a blanket inside the box to help them stay warm.

The entire time we were gone all I could think about was how cold it must be in that bathroom for my dog and her tiny puppies. When we returned two days later, it was freezing weather, and the ground was covered with snow. I raced inside and ran up the stairs to check on Frenchy and her puppies.

When I reached the doorway of the bathroom, I could see that one of the tiny puppies was lying on the floor, facing the back of the toilet. The little puppy had somehow fallen out of the box and had frozen to death on the cold tile of the bathroom floor.

Jami and I buried the tiny puppy, and we both grieved over the puppy's death.

We were furious at our uncle for refusing to heat the upstairs area and causing the puppy to freeze to death. A few days after we buried the puppy, I was on the couch in the living room and saw Frenchy coming out of our room toward me down the hallway. As I looked at Frenchy coming toward me, a thought came to me.

It dawned on me that the ghost Frenchy that I had seen before was not Frenchy at all, but instead it must have been the puppy that died. The ghost dog could have been the puppy because if she had grown up she would have looked just like Frenchy because she had her exact color and markings.

What led me to that belief was that when I had found the frozen puppy, she was lying in the exact spot where I had followed the ghost dog, right before it disappeared into thin air. I saw the ghost dog go to that spot three different times, and it disappeared right after it reached that spot. My theory was that maybe the ghost dog and our house had some kind of paranormal coexistence with death and the future.

5 | THE ATTACK OF THE BAT

OUR UNCLE HAD TO GO out of town for the weekend, and Tom came up from Las Vegas to watch over Jami and me. Honestly, I was glad he was going out of town because I was still so upset that I had lost the puppy. That evening we were all sitting at the kitchen table eating dinner and discussing the scary things that had happened in the house.

We didn't get very far in our discussion because all of a sudden from out of nowhere a bat dived from the ceiling and brushed through Tom's hair as it swept by. Tom was cussing and flailing his arms wildly in the air as Jami and I were just staring at that bizarre sight. Tom yelled, "What the hell . . . ? How did a bat get in the house?"

We didn't have any time to argue about how that bat had gotten into our house. The bat circled the room rapidly, diving and fiercely attacking each and every one of us. Tom grabbed a broom and started swatting at the bat, and he yelled to me to go to his room and get his 22 pistol, so I ran down the hallway to Tom's room, hoping that the bat wouldn't follow me. I got Tom's pistol and quickly brought it to him, and he started firing at the bat as it circled the room. Tom was really good with a gun, but he couldn't get a clean shot at the bat because it was flying so violently and erratically. Tom used up all of his ammunition and still could not got a clear shot at the bat.

Tom yelled to Jami and me to run to the downstairs room and that he would be right behind us. We all made it downstairs to the room and slammed the door shut behind us just in time.

We heard the bat fly into the door with a loud thud. It wasn't a single thud but many thuds repeated over and over, sounding much like someone punching the door with his fists. We couldn't believe that such a small bat could make such loud sounds as it repeatedly banged against the door over and over again. It literally sounded like the door was going to burst open under the intense pressure of the blows.

Tom reloaded his pistol with ammunition that he kept in his bag and then grabbed his car keys. Tom said, "If the door bursts open, we're going to make a run for the car and get the hell out of here." Just when we thought it was not going to end until the bat beat a hole through the door and came in through the hole to get us, the banging stopped and there was dead silence. It was the kind of silence in which you could hear a pin drop.

None of us said a word for fifteen or twenty minutes as we listened carefully for the slightest little sound that would indicate that the bat was outside the door waiting for us.

After a long while, Tom said, "I guess it must have killed itself banging into the door." We all decided to open the door and look outside, expecting to find a dead bat lying on the floor in the hallway. There was no bat outside the doorway, and there was no bat anywhere in the house. We searched the entire house in every nook and cranny but never found any sign of the bat.

We searched for places through where the bat could have gotten out of the house, but there was none, not even a tiny crack under a door where it could have squeezed through. We continued our search for days and weeks afterward, but we never found the bat or a place from where it could have escaped.

The door had so many dents on it. The door appeared as if someone had been pounding on it with his fists. The indentations were about the size of a tennis ball, which was much larger than what would be expected from a tiny bat striking the door. As we surveyed the damage to the door, which was extensive, we questioned how such a small bat, which was not much larger than a small mouse, could have done that type of damage to the door without harming or killing itself.

The ceiling also needed repairs after the incident because Tom had filled it with holes while firing at the bat with his pistol. The bat had vanished as quickly as it had appeared, and we never saw or heard from it again after that. I find it no longer a coincidence that the black bat was in the stairwell smashing against the downstairs door. Not long after the bat attacked us, I soon come face-to-face with something in the stairwell and was the scariest thing imaginable.

6 | THE FIGURE AT THE TOP OF THE STAIRS

I HAVE MENTIONED BEFORE THAT Jami and I felt uneasy and fearful when we went up or down the stairs, as did several of our friends and Tom. The time finally came when I discovered the reason for our fears. As I mentioned previously, the entity in that house liked to cause problems when you thought everything was safe and calm. This occurrence happened when I was not alone, and it happened during the day and not in the dark of the night when I would have expected it.

We were all getting ready to go to the home of one of our uncle's friends for a barbecue. Jami and my uncle were already downstairs getting ready to walk out the front door. I was upstairs alone in the kitchen waiting for my dog Frenchy to come out of our bedroom because I wanted to take her with us. Finally, she came out of the bedroom and walked into the kitchen, but she was acting strangely, shivering and crouching low to the floor and whimpering. When I reached out to pick her up, Frenchy resisted me and began to crawl backward away from me, as if she was afraid to come into the kitchen and living room area, which was located near the top of the staircase.

You will remember that I had written that she had behaved that way before, and it was very unlike Frenchy, who was a tough little dog that normally never showed any sign of fear.

I became angry with her and yelled out, "All right, you don't have to come with us." When I released her, she ran as fast as she could into my bedroom. I had written earlier of seeing Frenchy acting scared, but that was nothing compared to the way she was acting then. Frenchy was literally trembling with fear, and her behavior was beginning to scare me.

Frenchy was definitely detecting something that was very scary to her. I looked down the hallway, around the living room, and the kitchen to see what Frenchy was afraid of but saw nothing.

I heard Jami yelling at me from downstairs, "Let's go. We're waiting on you." So I put down Frenchy's leash and started down the stairs. As usual, I had that creepy uneasy feeling walking down the stairs, that feeling like someone was behind me watching me, but this time the feeling was stronger than ever before. In my mind, I began to associate Frenchy's fear with my own, and I got chills and goose bumps on my arms. As I neared the bottom of the stairs, the hair on the back of my neck stood up, and I could feel my heart racing. I could hear them yelling for me to hurry up and join them at the front door, but their calls didn't seem important to me at that moment.

Prompted by Frenchy's fearful behavior, that incident just became the most frightening moment that I had experienced since we had moved in. I had that intense and very positive feeling that I was being watched from behind. I mustered up enough courage to turn and look behind me.

I had never had the courage to look before, but that time it was a different situation. It was broad daylight, my family was in full view just a few feet away from me, standing at the front doorway waiting, and I felt like there was strength in numbers.

I decided that now was the perfect time to look behind me and dismiss the fears that had plagued me so many times in the past when I walked down those stairs.

As I stood at the base of the staircase, I turned slightly to the right so I could either direct my eyes to the left toward the front doorway or up and to the right toward the top square area of the staircase. As my gaze slowly moved from the floor and up the steps toward the top of the staircase, my eyes came upon the most incredibly frightening sight that the mind could conceive. I had one eye looking at Jami and one eye looking at the top of the stairs.

What I saw that day will forever be imprinted in my mind and will cause nightmares for the rest of my life.

Standing at the top of the staircase was an ominous dark and grotesque figure. I say a figure as I hesitate to call him a man or even a human.

The figure was cloaked completely in black with a dark hood that came over its head. The front edges of the hood were drawn in close around a hideous face that was unnaturally long and distorted and was a bloodless, cadaverous, ghostly white that made my skin crawl. The eyes were sunk way back into two large deep black holes, and they had a reddish glow to them.

The figure was holding a strange object, which looked like a pole or stick with a knife on the end.

The figure seemed very angry that I had turned and seen him. The figure held the pole with the knife on it with one hand while pointing at me with its other hand that was ghostly white in color and skeletal looking. He continued to stare at me with a look of hatred on his face. His mouth was filled with dirty, sharp spiked teeth with a hideous demonic grin.

I wanted to look away but couldn't. I started to cry, and tears were coming down my cheek as I was frozen in place. I couldn't breathe and I was not able to move any part of my body. My eyes were stuck on that thing and then on Jami. I was able to make eye contact with Jami as she stood in front of me. I remember just praying for Jami to help me. I didn't understand why I couldn't move. I was paralyzed with fear. The feeling of not being able to breathe was so horrifying as I stared at that thing. Jami was right there, and I just needed her to realize something was wrong. Jami looked at me, and then she started asking over and over, "Jodi, what's wrong?" When Jami saw my face turn white and saw the tears streaming down my face, Jami said that she knew something was wrong and she rushed to my side. As Jami reached me, she stretched out her arms and hugged me. I let out a huge gasp like someone who had almost drowned. As I turned my eyes upward toward the top of the stairs where the figure had been, I saw nothing; it had vanished. I was still frozen with fear as Jami pulled me through the doorway at the bottom of the stairs. Jami rushed me along and out of the front door where our uncle was waiting by the SUV.

The next fifteen minutes was spent with Jami trying to calm me down from the hysteria I was experiencing. Eventually, I was able to talk and tell her what I had seen. As expected, our uncle scoffed at my story of what I had just witnessed. Jami knew what I had told her was the truth and she had seen the way I had looked at the doorway. I tried to describe what I had seen, but it was hard to do that with our uncle irritated at me for crying. My uncle's main concern was for all of us to get into the car so we could go to the party.

At the time, I had no idea about what I had seen. A few days later after relaying the story to my friends at school and describing what I had seen, I saw a drawing on my friend's school folder. When I saw the picture, I screamed out, "That's it. That's what I saw."

He said, "Do you know what that is?" When I said no, he said, "That's the Grim Reaper." I asked him to explain, and he said, "It's the figure of death. They say he comes to get people and take them away when they die." Everyone was horrified when I explained to them that I had actually seen the figure in my house. The friend who had drawn the image said to me, "That's just a legend. It's not real." My friend was so wrong; that thing did exist!

I did some research and came to the conclusion that what I had seen was indeed the Grim Reaper, sometimes called the Angel of Death, who is the personification of death that has been passed on through folklore and documented and talked about for centuries. I never saw that figure again, nor did I understand why I had seen it. Thinking about that figure made me constantly worry that I or someone close to me was going to die.

7 | THE FEAR NEXT DOOR

IT WOULD TURN OUT THAT our house wasn't the only one in the neighborhood where scary things were happening. Our neighbor in the house next door to ours was about to experience something supernatural and life-threatening. Our next-door neighbor was named Al, who had built his dream retirement home for him and his golden retriever on the lot next to our house. The lot sizes in our area of Big Bear were mostly small, maybe fifty feet by hundred feet, so our house was very close to Al's.

It was approaching dusk, and Jami and I were eating dinner at home by ourselves. The house was quiet, and we didn't hear anything or smell anything out of the ordinary. Then, all of a sudden, we heard a fire truck. We ran outside and the fire truck stopped in front of Al's house, and we saw smoke pouring out of its windows. The firefighters went inside, and fortunately they were able to put out the fire and prevented Al's house from burning to the ground.

When we were able to talk to Al, he was both angry and scared. We asked him what had happened, and Al yelled angrily at me and Jami, blaming us for not helping him in his time of need.

He said, "Why didn't you help me? I was right there on my porch with my dog, screaming at the top of my lungs for help? You were in your house, not more than fifty feet away, and you didn't so much as come outside to see what was happening." We couldn't believe how mad Al was; he was furious as he scolded us. We told Al how sorry we were and told him that we didn't hear a thing.

Al just became angrier, and he said, "How in the hell did you not see or smell the smoke? Someone called in the fire alarm from two blocks away, and your house is right there." He pointed at our house. We continued to tell him that we had heard nothing, and finally Al started to calm down.

We asked him what happened, and that was when Al began to act really scared. He was shaking and almost in tears when he said, "It was a fire that just came out of nowhere. It was not there and then it was, and it acted like it had a mind of its own and it literally chased us out of the house." He meant his dog and him. "We ran out the back door onto the porch, and I slammed the door behind us to stop the fire."

Al was right; Jami and I had no idea how we couldn't have noticed the fire or not have heard him screaming. Whatever happened in Al's house had him so scared that soon after he packed up all of his things and moved away from Big Bear, leaving his perfect dream home behind, and he never returned. We never saw Al again. I believe that there was more to that fire incident than what he had told us. Al had spent so much money on his dream home, and to think that he fled his house and town over a bizarre fire didn't make sense. There had to be more to that fire than he had told us. Al was a hunter and tough mountain guy who wouldn't scare easily. I've often wondered what it was that he was holding back.

8 | THE SPIRIT BOARD

WE HAD HEARD THAT THE Spirit Board would let us communicate with the supernatural world, and we had lots of questions about our house and the hauntings. So Jami and I saved and pooled our money and bought one at one of the local stores. We brought the box home to try out. It was getting dusk when we brought the board home with us still unopened in its box.

Jami and I moved the giant braided circular rug from the downstairs area to upstairs right in front of the fireplace. Next to the rug by the fireplace was a strange-looking small antique table with a small storage compartment and a door with ornamental design underneath. On the top of the table was an antique lamp with three crystal ornaments dangling in a circular ring below the light fixture. The dim light coming from the antique lamp on the table, the light from the antique kerosene lamp on the mantel above the fireplace, and the light from the flickering fire in the fireplace provided the only light in the room, as Jami and I sat on the rug, opened the Spirit Board box, and began to read the instructions for its use. The only other light source in the upstairs area was the light bulb hanging from the ceiling, but we had turned that one off with its pull chain.

The setting was perfect for a scary night conducting a spirit-seeking session. We were in the upstairs area of a house that already terrified us, and the dim lighting, the flickering fire, and the usual silence that is the norm in a cabin in a remote area of the forest during the middle of the night kept us alert and constantly looking over our shoulders.

We didn't waste much time in getting into it. We sat facing each other on the giant round braided rug with the board between us and our fingers lightly touching the Spirit Board and the movement piece. It was twenty-six-years ago that that happened, so I don't remember the exact questions we asked it and the exact order that we asked them, but here is a close approximation of what we asked. We asked the board random questions such as: "Is there anyone here?" "What's your name?" "Who are you?" We did ask what its name was, but I don't remember what it spelled out.

All of a sudden, the movement piece started darting around the board quickly and violently, spelling out violent words and profanities. The Spirit Board was going nuts, and it was scaring Jami and me, so we folded up the board and put it back inside its box. We placed the box inside the antique table that was in front of the fireplace. After what happened, neither one of us got a wink of sleep that night.

The next morning, we agreed that we should never use it again, so we decided to throw it away. I opened the door in the antique table and took the Spirit Board out, and both Jami and I carried it out to the trash can that we had set out for the trash pickup, which was scheduled for that day. Later that day, we heard the noise of the garbage truck down the street approaching our house, so Jami and I nervously went to the window to watch the truck arrive at our house.

The garbage truck pulled up out front, and one of the sanitation workers took the lid off the can and dumped its contents inside the garbage truck, before the truck proceeded down the street to the next house. Jami and I breathed a sigh of relief that the Spirit Board was now gone.

A few days later, I was preparing to start the fire in the fireplace, so I went to the antique table and opened the door underneath to get out the lighter fluid and matches that we kept in there. As I opened the cabinet, my heart must have skipped a beat, as I struggled to catch my breath. There in front of me was an unbelievable and horrifying sight. The Spirit Board box was back in its place, just like we had placed it on the first night.

Jami heard me gasp, saw my reaction, and quickly came to my side, and her eyes cautiously followed mine down to the box inside the table. I asked Jami, "Did you take the box out of the trash?"

She said, "No, I didn't, did you take it out?" We argued back and forth for a minute, and she said, "This isn't possible. You know we both saw it go into our trash can, and we both saw the garbage truck drive off with our trash inside." Once we both calmed down enough to catch our breath and talk, we took the box out of the table, opened it, and inspected the contents.

Jami said, "It's impossible. We threw it away, but it's here!"

I looked inside the box and said, "This is it. This is the same box. Everything is in the same place where we put it the first time." Jami yelled out, "We have to burn it. That's the only way!" I took the lighter fluid and matches out of the table, and we soaked the box and its contents with lighter fluid, threw it into the fireplace, and set fire to it.

Jami and I sat there on the rug silent and terrified for about ten minutes, watching the Spirit Board burn into ashes. We had heard stories about people burning their boards and hearing screams come from the fire. We heard no screams that day, and it's good that we didn't. I believe that hearing screams come from that burning Spirit Board would have sent us both over the edge.

9 | THINGS WERE MOVING

I WAS SITTING ON THE green braided rug with my dog, Frenchy, in front of the fireplace trying to get a little bit of warmth from the fire. As I sat there petting Frenchy and gazing into the fire, I heard a tinkling sound. I looked around the room, and finally my gaze focused on the lamp. The three dangling crystals attached to the lamp were starting to sway gently in a circular pattern, and they were hitting the sides of the center portion of the lamp, making the tinkling sound that I had been hearing.

As you might imagine, that was terrifying for me because there was no reasonable explanation for what I was seeing. There were no fans to cause air flow in the rooms. Other than the sound of the crystals brushing up against the lamp, the room was still and quiet.

I was frozen in place, holding Frenchy tightly in my lap, and unable to talk or cry out to Jami, who was down the hall inside our bedroom. All of a sudden, it was as if something was becoming very violent and was trying to scare me. Sitting there was terrifying, watching the crystals moving; I was definitely scared. The dangling crystals began shaking violently and moving erratically, not hanging vertically but instead blowing straight out. The dangling crystals were swaying as if they were in a high wind, yet there was no breeze in the house.

That scared me even more than before because I realized that my presence there was making something very upset. I was afraid that whatever was causing that to happen would take out their anger on me physically. Frenchy was whimpering and struggling to get free of my grasp. She wanted to get as far away from there as possible.

Finally, I stood up and ran to my bedroom, carrying Frenchy with me, slamming the door behind me. Jami asked me what had happened and she tried to calm me down. As soon as I caught my breath, stopped shaking, and was able to talk, I started telling Jami what had happened. That occurred during one of the times that Tom was visiting from Las Vegas, and he heard us talking from his room down the hall. Tom came into our room and listened as I was telling Jami what had happened. After a few minutes, the three of us went into the living room and over to the fireplace to look at the lamp, which was now quite still as if nothing had happened. I knew what I had seen had occurred. It was just like when Tom tried to catch a glimpse of what was turning on every light upstairs instantaneously, yet he couldn't see it. The dangling crystals were then perfectly still, and I was now terrified of that lamp.

10 | THE JAMI GHOST

ONE OF THE THINGS THAT Jami and I both enjoyed doing a lot was watching music videos on TV. One day, Jami and I were home alone, and our stepfather was still at work. I was upstairs watching videos and sitting on the couch with my dog Frenchy.

Frenchy jumped off my lap and went into our bedroom, which was just a few feet away down the hallway. I thought that Frenchy must have gone there to take a nap. She liked to sleep at the end of my bed or on my pillow.

The TV DJ announced that a new music video would be coming up shortly. Jami was downstairs doing something, so I yelled down to her, telling her to come upstairs to see the new video. She ignored my calls and didn't answer, and that made me mad. I yelled again, "Jami, hurry get up here." Jami still did not answer me, and she still did not come upstairs. The video started, and I yelled downstairs to her one more time, "That's it, Jami. What's wrong with you?" Suddenly, out of the corner of my eye, I caught a glimpse of Jami, and I turned toward Jami and said, "What's wrong with you? Why wouldn't you listen to me?" As I looked at Jami and scolded her, I didn't realize it at that moment but something really scary was happening. The Jami I was scolding was not the fifteen-year-old

Jami I knew, yet I was sure that it was Jami. The Jami I was scolding had hair that was blonde and long, not medium brown with the bob cut that we both wore at the time, and she seemed to be older and much thinner, almost like someone suffering from severe anorexia. She was visibly quite different, and yet I still knew it was Jami, and I didn't even notice the physical difference. She was wearing a peach-colored dress that came down to her knees, and it was a very loose flowing-type fabric with slits on the sleeve, and she had on short, thin white bootie socks that looked brand new. Neither one of us owned a peach-colored dress, and all of our socks were old, frayed, threadbare, and worn out. Neither Jami nor I had a dress of that color and appearance.

It all happened so fast that I didn't have time to wonder why her appearance had changed so radically, but I knew it was Jami, in spite of how different she looked. The couch I was sitting on was lined up with the hallway to our bedroom on the right, toward the bathroom across the hall to the left, and Tom's room just a little farther down the hallway on the left. Jami had just come up the step that was visible on entering the living room.

When I first saw Jami, she turned her face away from me so I couldn't see it. I thought it was odd that Jami was walking right past me and wouldn't answer me and was avoiding looking at me too! I said, "Would you just stop!" When I said that, Jami stopped dead in her tracks, as if my words finally got to her. She stopped and paused, looking straight ahead only for a couple of seconds. Jami was standing right next to me not more than three inches away from me. Jami was physically solid and whole, just as regular as a normal living and breathing human being.

I was waiting for Jami to turn and look at me and say something, but she didn't. Instead, she continued walking so slowly toward the hallway without turning around. There was something strange about the way she was walking. Jami was walking abnormally slow and methodically, taking small steps, and not walking the normal way that Jami would walk. She was totally ignoring me, even though I kept yelling, "Stop! Jami, please stop!" Jami ignored me and kept on walking, and that was making me upset.

I must have yelled "stop" five or six times, and she did not respond. She reached the door to our bedroom and paused for a couple of seconds before entering our bedroom. Jami stood there, staring straight ahead into the bedroom from the doorway. She just stood there staring and gazing into our bedroom from the doorway. Jami stood there without any movement and was completely frozen and motionless as she looked through the doorway. Then all of a sudden, Jami just walked right through the door and was gone out of my sight.

It was at that exact moment that I saw something out of the corner of my eye that shocked me senseless and scared the living daylights out of me. As I saw Jami entering through the door into our bedroom, I could also see to the right that Jami had reached the top of the staircase and was entering the living room area at the exact same time. Jami was asking me what I was yelling about. I did a double take, looking at Jami in the living room and looking at the door to our bedroom where I had just seen Jami entering.

I froze in terror and had difficulty in breathing, just as I had done when I had seen the dark figure at the top of the stairs before. Again, Jami recognized my fear and my difficulty in breathing and came to my side to help me calm down. She asked me what was wrong, and I told Jami what I had just witnessed. When Jami realized what I was saying, she became just as frightened as I was, and she said, "Let's get out of here!" We started running down the stairs, outside, jumped on our bikes, and rode into the forest where we liked to hang out.

In the forest, there was this breathtaking area that consisted of a large cluster of boulders that seemed to be out of place. The boulders were just there right in the middle of the forest, and you could walk on them and lie on them. Those boulders were almost as if they were placed in that area of the forest intentionally. There was also a stream that ran year round on the way to the boulders.

Many times when Jami and I would go to the forest where the boulders were, we were met by these two hybrid dogs. The two dogs would usually be at the entrance of the path that led to the boulders in the forest. The two massive dogs were unlike any other dogs we had ever seen before or even till now. The dogs looked like part wolf and part Samoyed. The wolf hybrids were huge, and they dwarfed the size of a full-blooded wolf.

I remember the first time we saw them. Honestly, we were so scared the first time they appeared right in front of us from out of nowhere. We assumed they had come from the forest. Those wolf hybrids were the largest dogs imaginable. The wolf hybrids were the size of great Danes with the look of a white and silver wolf and the heavy thick coat of a Samoyed. If we ran from those huge wolf hybrids, we knew that we would probably be attacked. I looked at Jami and said, "We better try to see if those dogs can be friendly because we can't outrun them."

Jami and I stared at those amazing wolf hybrids and walked slowly with our hands down, our palms showing, and called out to them to come over to us. Luckily Jami and I had packed sack lunches to eat in the forest. We opened up one of the bags, took out some food, and placed it on the palm of our hands. The wolf hybrids stared at us, and then slowly we walked toward them and they walked toward us. They were not scared of us; they walked with their heads held high and so gracefully with such amazing powerful presence. We were then finally face-to-face with the wolf hybrids, and they let us both pet them briefly as they ate the food we had in our hands. The fur on the wolf hybrids was unlike any dog's fur I had ever felt. The fur was so thick that you couldn't get your hands through all the thick fur to even feel their backs. That was really odd; it was like they were just solid muscular fur. The wolf hybrids let us walk past them to get to the boulder area in the forest. From that day on, whenever we went to that location, we were usually greeted by those amazing wolf hybrids .I always got a pit in my stomach when I saw the hybrids because they were so massively huge .It was as if the wolf hybrids were guarding the entrance to the forest where the boulders were. That area of the forest was so peaceful and serene .I have since found out that there are two known Indian Burial grounds in Big Bear. The Indians who lived and hunted in the area cremated there deceased loved ones and scattered the ashes in areas that had large boulder structured areas .I plan on making a trip back to that area to look for any signs that could indicate if that area was possibly an ancient Indian Burial ground.

When Jami and I finally returned home from the forest after meeting the wolf hybrids for the first time, we were very frightened to be upstairs alone with whatever was in that house. Jami and I went together into the bedroom and looked around. We looked in the closet and under the bed, but the ghost Jami had vanished and we were glad that she had. Jami and I looked at each other, and we knew what the other one was thinking.

We both knew that it was going to be another one of those nights when neither of us would get any sleep. Jami and I had then reached the point that I slept in the bottom bunk bed with Jami. I was now too scared to sleep alone. We would drape my blankets from the top bunk to make a curtain surrounding the bottom bunk bed. We figured that there was a ghost in that house, and I didn't want to see it again. So with the entire bottom bunk bed enclosed, we felt safe from what was outside the blankets.

Jami and I stayed in our bedroom waiting for our uncle to go to sleep. We were not about to spend the night in that house, and as soon as our uncle went to sleep, we were going outside to spend the night in our tree house. We talked most of the night while sitting on the ground in our room, just talking about what was happening in the house. We remembered the incident where I had seen the dog that I thought was Frenchy, but it too was a ghost that disappeared into thin air, just as the Jami ghost did after entering our bedroom. We had also come to the conclusion that the Frenchy ghost was somehow really a glimpse into the future, showing us that one of Frenchy's pups would someday freeze to death behind the toilet in the bathroom, where I saw the ghost dog go twice before disappearing.

Recalling the ghost dog incident was a very frightening thought to me because I hoped that seeing the Jami ghost was not a glimpse into the future about the death of Jami. When I suggested that to Jami, she became frightened, and I told her that maybe there was something we could do to prevent something bad from happening to her. Perhaps we could have saved Frenchy's pup if we had just kept the pups out of the bathroom, where the pup eventually froze to death.

I suggested that we needed to make sure that she never even owned any clothing that was peach colored much less that peach dress she was in. The ghost was also wearing a particular kind of white bootie socks, so we agreed that Jami would never wear that kind either. From that point on, I made it my permanent job to protect Jami, and the best way that I knew how to do that was to prevent her from wearing those clothes.

The ghost Jami looked so young, maybe eighteen to twenty-eight years old, and secretly that scared me that Jami could die young. It wasn't until years later that I fully understood the true significance of the ghost Jami incident and the ghost Frenchy incident, but I did finally understand.

11 | THE MUD ROOM

EARLIER, I MENTIONED THAT WHEN we first arrived at the house for the first time, there was a curious room located at the base of the staircase directly across from our uncle's bedroom. Jami and I called that room the Mud Room because the room was not a room at all but a small crude storage area that jutted out against the hillside and constructed with a little bit of lumber, a doorway into the house. The largest portion of the floors and walls was actually the dirt of the hillside, which was always damp and packed with mud.

The room was a small unfinished room that was very dark and spooky, and there were no lights in that room. To see in the room, we had to leave the door open into the hallway at the base of the stairs to let a little light into the room. We used the room to store things that we didn't really care about, like tools, lawn equipment, Christmas decorations, storage boxes, etc. That room reminded us of the scary movies where someone was held against their will and locked in a cellar or underground area from where they couldn't possibly escape. I hated to even go in the room because it gave me an eerie feeling and made me keep looking over my shoulder to make sure that the door wasn't closing behind me to trap me inside.

There was no way that the door could close and lock me inside, but I still had that scary feeling anyway.

One day our uncle asked Jami and me to put some Christmas decorations and other miscellaneous things into the room. The room was getting full, so Jami and I got some shovels and started digging into the slanted dirt wall at the back of the room against the hillside to make more room for stacking boxes. While Jami was digging, she uncovered something interesting and asked me to take a look. It was a large bone that looked like it could be human. To me, it looked like it was about the size of a forearm bone, the one between the wrist and the elbow.

We went upstairs and got Tom to come down and look at it, and he said it looked more like a femur because it was so large. That room creeped Tom out also, so he wanted to get out of there as soon as he could too. I asked Tom what were we going to do with the bone, and he said that we definitely were not going to leave it there. I don't know who disposed of the bone or if it was human or not.

We all wondered about where that bone came from and about what else may have been buried in that room. We wondered if something could be lying beneath the ground in that Mud Room. Maybe the bone had something to do with the scary things we were all experiencing. Tom had witnessed and fallen victim to many scary events, feelings, and accidents. Tom almost lost his life in that house due to the freak accidents. Tom told us that he had to drive back to Las Vegas for a few days and that our uncle had to go out of town for a work-related event. Tom wanted us to stay calm, and he let us know that he would be back soon. Staying calm was pretty much impossible in that house. It seemed like an eternity before Tom returned. It was terrifying to think of just the two of us upstairs without Tom.

12 | THE THING OUTSIDE THE DOOR

O UR UNCLE WAS GOING TO be gone for a day, and he had asked a
female friend of his to stay with us. Even though Jami and I were in
our teens and well equipped to take care of ourselves, our uncle wanted
someone to be there with us when he was away, especially since we lived
in a remote area. His friend's name was Kim, and she was an attractive
woman in her early forties and a single parent. We wondered why our
uncle wasn't dating her, and looking back now, maybe he was and we just
didn't know it.

Kim brought along her son, Trey, who was about our same age—
around fifteen years old. Our uncle had told Kim to make by herself at
home in the comfort of his room downstairs, where she could watch cable
TV, read, or just relax. Jami and I invited her son, Trey, upstairs to play
board games with us in our room. When this incident occurred, Tom
wasn't visiting from Las Vegas, so his room down the hall was empty, and
it was very quiet upstairs. We could faintly hear the sound coming from
our uncle's TV downstairs, but that was all we could hear. The three of
us were sitting on the floor playing a board game with the door to our
room closed, just like always. Jami and I now always made sure our door
was shut.

We didn't tell Trey anything about the eerie things we had been experiencing there because, first of all, we knew Trey would have taunted and teased us if we had told him. Trey was a very disturbed boy. He was into very bad and evil things. He was a bully, and he loved to torture animals till they died. We had watched him one time get his kitten and walk over to the fireplace, and out of nowhere, he had thrown that little kitten into the fire. The cat screamed and ran out of the fireplace on fire. I don't know if the kitten lived or not. Trey was just a very scary kid who was capable of seriously hurting others; even his mother was scared of him.

A few minutes after we had started playing a game, we heard a man's voice outside our door. We thought that our uncle had come home, and he was playing a joke on us. The voice said in a scary kind of way, "I'm going to kill you!" Then we heard the sound of a chain dragging on the wooden floor and heard it clanging against our door. Again we heard the voice say, "Let me in now!" Thinking it was our uncle, we all started laughing. Then all hell broke loose with the sound of the chain banging against the door, the sound of a fist pounding on the door, and the sound of the doorknob being twisted violently. We could see the doorknob turning and wobbling. Our hallway was not very wide, and the sounds were amplified down the hallway and outside our door.

What a time for Tom to not be there visiting! Jami and I had come to depend on him to protect us when he was staying with us, but he was gone and Trey was no help at all. Trey was screaming repeatedly, "Mom . . . Mom . . . Mom!" Trey's screaming seemed to make whatever it was on the other side of the door madder because his voice got louder, repeating that he was going to get us, and the pounding on the door and the shaking of the doorknob became more violent.

By that time, all three of us were frightened out of our wits and screaming at the top of our lungs and crying. Then all of a sudden, things got really quiet, and we stopped our screaming to listen if we could hear any movement on the other side of the door. We all huddled in the corner of the bed, staring at the door. Slowly we saw the doorknob twisting and the door opening just a crack right before it started to swing open. I'm sure we all turned white as a sheet as we looked in anticipation at what might be coming through the door, possibly to kill us.

As the door opened fully, we saw that it was Kim, and she looked very angry. When she entered our bedroom, Trey jumped up and ran to his mom crying, and she took him in her arms and said, "What's wrong? Why is Trey crying? What was all the commotion?"

We were all crying and relieved to see Kim. We told her, "Something was just outside our door! Something was going to kill us! There really was something. We're not lying!"

Kim didn't know what to think of that situation and was angry at Trey, thinking that maybe he had been scaring or hurting me and Jami.

Kim took Trey back downstairs to stay with her for the rest of the night. The next day our uncle returned home. I'm sure that Trey told his mom of what had happened. Trey's mom, I think believed him, because neither one of them ever returned to our house again after that. We saw Trey at school a few days later, and he told us he was convinced that there was something supernatural and very dangerous about our house, and he was sorry that Jami and I had to stay there and live with it.

That was a side of Trey that not many people saw. He was the tough, mean bully who as a kid one would be scared to be near. Things had changed between the three of us. Trey never spoke of what happened at our house again, and he left us alone and never bullied us anymore. I think Trey actually felt sorry for us. Trey proudly admitted to worshipping the devil and doing horrible things to people and animals. Trey realized that that devil he was worshipping was not what he had thought. It was interesting how he was so into animal sacrifice and devil worship, yet when we were in our room he didn't pray for the devil to save him. Trey was praying "Oh my god, help me." For Trey, devil worshipping was cool to him, and to be confronted by a demon on the other side of the door, well let's just say, I think he changed his religion.

The next day after school, I was outside with a steak knife making a sharp-tipped stick for protection when Jami and I hiked through the woods. Jami and I had carved many of those before. I found the stick I wanted to use and sat down outside on a log where Tom had been hurt in the wood splitting incident. The stick was face down as I sharpened the tip with the steak knife. I kept slicing downward over and over again till the end was very sharp.

This is the part I don't understand as I was sharpening the stick. For some reason, I decided to do one more slice to sharpen it, and I took the knife, and instead of cutting the tip downward like always, I sliced upward toward me. I was using as much strength as I could to push down and put pressure on the knife as I started to cut. To my horror, it was as if I was watching my body harm itself and I couldn't stop it. I placed the knife on the tip of the stick and started to cut upward towards my thumb. To my horror I started to cut my entire left thumb wide open. Blood started gushing out of my hand, and all I could do was stare at my uncontrollable right hand with the knife cutting my left thumb. The knife cut didn't hurt as it was happening; I didn't feel anything. Then I dropped the knife, and it fell down to the dirt ground.Instantly I was in so much pain. I looked at my thumb as it gushed blood onto the dirt. I and ran up the backstairs to the upstairs kitchen sink. Quickly i started to rinse my hand off and to see how bad the damage was to my thumb. I moved the skin to apply pressure, hoping to stop the bleeding. As I put the towel on my thumb, all of the skin flopped over and there was my entire bone showing through the blood that was still coming out. I called for Jami to come to the kitchen, and I showed her what I had done and how it had happened. My thumb bled for hours. My uncle wasn't going to be home till the evening and Tom was not there that weekend. I was afraid to call my uncle and tell him because he would lose hours of work and he would get mad at me, so I waited till he got off work and came home to show him my thumb. My uncle came home, and I went up to him and told him that I had accidentally cut myself earlier in the morning; he asked me to unveil the bandage on my thumb so he could see how bad it was.

Then he saw that my thumb had been cut down to the bone and that the length of my entire thumb was really in bad shape. I was starting to not feel good like I was going to faint. I hadn't felt that way earlier. My thumb had been bleeding a lot for hours, and my uncle said that we needed to get to the Emergency Room right away.

We arrived at the Emergency Room, and I was sitting on the hospital bed when the Doctor came in and started checking the depth of the cut. The Doctor looked at my uncle and said that I had waited too long to come to the hospital and that he didn't know if he could save my thumb. The Doctor went to get a needle, then he lifted up the skin to where the bone was showing and gave me the most painful shot I had ever had. He had to numb my thumb to stitch it up, and that was the only way to numb me properly. I screamed and cried so hard when he injected that shot.

Then the Doctor threaded some black wire-type string and started stitching me up. It was so bizarre watching him stitch it closed. The Doctor also gave me antibiotics because he feared that infection had set in. He told me and my uncle that if the thumb started to form pus or if I developed a fever, he would have to amputate my thumb. I was so distraught over the entire situation. My hand was in so much pain when the anesthesia wore off. The Doctor told me that when the anesthesia wore off I should just take Asprin. Well, Asprin didn't help the pain at all. The Doctor was a jerk,he knew I was going to be in a lot of pain real soon but I didnt.I was so miserable for the next few days.

I still didn't understand how I had done that to myself and how come it didn't hurt when I was cutting open my thumb with that steak knife. The pain didn't even hit me till the knife dropped to the ground. None of it made sense to me about that entire situation. I was so worried about getting an infection that I would put my thumb over the sink and pour alcohol over it and scream because of the intense burning pain. I did that a few times a day for a week till my thumb looked better. The alcohol did its job; my thumb never became infected. I was so traumatized from enduring all of that pain during that week. The entire situation was horrible. I now have a long scar there now, and it's a constant reminder of that day.

During that time, the weather began to set records with rainfall and damages. I had never seen anything like that before. Huge pine trees fell over and landed on people's homes because of the high winds. Little dry streams or washes became torrential raging rivers that engulfed anything in its path. I remember reading in the paper that a little girl had been outside on her home's deck watching the rain. It turned out that their house backed against a wash. Out of nowhere, a huge wave of water came rushing down the wash and engulfed the little girl's deck, carrying her away in the raging water. What a horrible story to read! I knew the area where she lived and had walked down the wash many times before. Jami and I saw photos of how the wash looked when she was carried away and later found dead. There was so much water, mud, and debris. I didn't know that a wash could turn deadly because of rain. From that time on, whenever it rained we made sure we were not near any small creeks or washes because we had seen what they turned into with large amounts of rainfall.

The entire town felt terrible for the little girl and her family. That was such a tragic accident. After living through such a weird season, I now understand how dangerous and unpredictable rain can be. That season was so bizarre with the plague of frogs and the wild weather. That all coincided with the more traumatic events unfolding in our home.

13 | TOM AND THE MOTORCYCLE

Tom was back from Las Vegas visiting us again. Tom was always such a relief to have in the house. One day, Tom rode his motorcycle down to the store to grab a few groceries. It was toward the late afternoon, and then we heard sirens and fire trucks very close to the house. Jami and I ran outside to see if we could see anything, and it turned out Tom was on the ground and had crashed his motorcycle. There were people around him, trying to keep him still, and there was a girl around ten years old on the ground next to her bike, and she was bleeding from her leg. The ambulance came roaring down the street with the sirens and lights on. The paramedics took Tom to the hospital where they put him in a medically induced coma for two weeks. No one had any idea of why or what had exactly happened to cause the crash.Unexpectedly one day Tom opened his eyes and started screaming from the pain throughout his body. He had suffered major injuries, and not even the Doctors knew how to handle the numerous traumas throughout his body.Tom awoke to find himself in a room with other men who were in as serious condition as himself from crashes. When Tom was stable and able to talk about the crash, we found out how it had occurred.

Tom had been just coming down the street and doing around 25 mph when he saw two girls on their bikes further down our street. He beeped the horn on his motorcycle, and the girls pulled over on their bicycles. Just as Tom was ready to pass them, one of the girls got back on her bike and drove right in front of Tom and stopped. Tom only had seconds to react. He ditched the bike and laid it down or he would have killed her for sure, he said.

In the 1980s, helmets were not a Law, and most people did not wear them. So when Tom crashed, he hit the pavement headfirst with his motorcycle rolling on him too. The little girl was hit on her lower leg area and required stitches.

To this day, Tom has no idea what made that girl just drive right in front of him when she had been at the curb waiting for him to pass. Tom said he remembered that she just had a blank look on her face as she rode her bike and stopped in front of him. It made no sense why the little girl did that. It was almost as if she was in some form of a trance and not in control of what she was doing by riding directly into the path of Tom and then stopping.It took Tom weeks to recover from so many injuries.

14 | THE GRAVEYARD

OUR UNCLE HAD TO GO out of town for another meeting. As you have read, that happened a few times throughout the year. This time he left a woman named Samantha to watch over us. Jami and I had told her a few of the stories of what had happened to us in the house, and it turned out that she believed in the paranormal. Samantha asked Jami and me if we knew of the old graveyard in Big Bear City by the old Gold mine. We had never heard of that before and really didn't believe her. We figured that she was just telling us scary stories about some fake old miners' graveyard to scare us. Jami and I told her that if it was true, then to show us because we had never heard of that place.

All three of us got in her car and drove out to the area that she said was where the cemetery was located. We looked and didn't see anything remotely like a cemetery. We all got out of the car and took a little hike to the area that she was leading us to. The area was covered with lots of rocks that were orange in color and bushes. We walked toward the area, slipping on the rocks covering the ground.

We hiked briefly; then as we looked ahead, there was an old white cross next to a tree. Samantha said, "Well, this is it." Jami and I looked around, and you could see sparse rock formations where bodies were buried and a few old wooden crosses. She was right; it was some kind of cemetery. Maybe it was a pet cemetery or just an area that was made to look like an old graveyard.

We just didn't believe that we had spent so many years in Big Bear and not heard of that place. Jami and I looked at the rock markers, and then Jami looked at me and said, "I still don't believe it. I am going to dig a bit and see if anything's under all these rocks."

I told her, "I am not touching anything. What if it's real?" So Jami started digging for just a few minutes, and then there it was—a bone from a jaw. Samantha looked over and asked what we were doing; she said that she wanted to leave. I told Jami to drop the bone and we went back to the car.

As we sat in the backseat, Jami opened her pocket and showed me the bone. I was so scared to even have that thing in the car much less know that we had touched someone's sacred burial ground. I had thought Jami had put it down; I had no idea she had put it in her pocket. We went home, and I told Jami that we couldn't keep that bone and it was wrong that she had it with her. We went to Samantha and showed the bone to her, and she flipped out and chewed us out for doing that, which Jami did have it coming. She took the bone from Jami and told us to stay at the house, and then she got in the car and drove back to the graveyard.

When she returned, Samantha lectured us on ghosts, spirits, final resting places, and the morals that Jami had broken. Jami felt horrible for taking the bone. Jami and I both prayed that night for forgiveness and that we were sorry for even going there to the graveyard, for walking on that sacred ground, and for Jami taking the bone.

15 | TOM'S VISIT AND HIS CAT

TOM HAD DRIVEN BACK TO Las Vegas and brought his new girlfriend and her calico cat up to Big Bear for all of us to meet. We all enjoyed meeting Tom's new girlfriend and having just a great night of fun and laughter. As it started to get late, it was time for Jami and me to go to bed. We actually slept pretty well that night.

Before we knew it, morning was here. It was about six in the morning; Jami and I woke up early because Tom came into our room and woke us up. Tom told us that he had to leave and go back to Las Vegas right away. He didn't explain why, and his girlfriend was already in the car at that point ready to leave. We didn't get the chance to say good-bye to her or her cat. The entire situation was weird. I never knew what happened to make Tom leave so abruptly till I started writing this book.

I spoke to Tom recently, and he explained what had happened. Our uncle had opened his door to go to work at around 6:00 a.m., and when he opened the door, he almost tripped. He looked down at his feet to see what he had tripped on, and it was Tom's cat. The cat had been ripped to shreds. Her stomach was almost completely ripped open, and she had organs just hanging out of her. My uncle ran upstairs to get Tom and his girlfriend. They were all shocked at how that cat could be so torn apart.

That seemed strategic, as if the cat was placed right there at the front door as a gruesome warning. If the cat had been attacked by a coyote, the cat would never have made it home. The cat was still alive but dying. A coyote would have just taken the cat and finished the poor thing as a meal. It made no sense that the cat was slowly and painfully dying on the doorstep.

No one even knew how the cat got out in the first place. We also had our dogs, and they never barked once. If the cat was being attacked by wild animals, our dogs would have alerted us by barking full blast. The cat was taken to the veterinarian where it died. Tom's girlfriend was so distraught that she insisted she wanted to leave the house immediately and get out of Big Bear.

16 | JAMI AND THE BOTTOM BUNK BED

IT WAS TIME TO GO to bed, and I had decided to sleep on the top bunk while Jami took the bottom. We had now begun to sleep with our lights on. It wasn't very long into trying to fall asleep when I heard Jami scream. Jami started screaming, "There's someone under my bed." I looked down from the top bunk, and Jami was backed into the corner of the bed with her blankets pulled up around her. She was so scared. Then I was scared too. I couldn't just leave her there and I didn't want to hop off the top bunk onto the ground if there was something under her bed. So I slid down the bed onto hers without touching the ground.

I asked Jami what was it that had caused her to scream. Jami told me that she had been still wide awake and she had her hand dangling over the bed. She said that all of a sudden sharp fingernails had clawed her hand right up to her arm as if scratching her. Jami was positive that something with sharp fingernails had clawed at her arm. We eventually looked under the bed, and nothing was there. Never again did Jami or I let a foot or hand hang off the bed. I still don't, even though I am an adult now.

17 | MOVING OUT

OUR UNCLE HAD LOST THE home and it was in foreclosure. We were going to move to another house in Big Bear. Jami and I were so relieved. The time we had spent in that house had traumatized us for life. As far as I was concerned, we couldn't get our stuff out of there fast enough. We had Tom, our uncle, and some other men helping move the last heavy items into the SUV. We were then down to the last heavy item to load. The item was a solid heavy one-piece antique Barber's Chair. My uncle moved the chair in with Tom when he purchased it. They both had no problem moving the chair other than it was heavy.

We were all outside as Tom, my uncle, and two other men were lifting the Barber's Chair into the SUV.

As we watched them carrying the chair, a tragic accident occurred. The guys were all lifting the heavy Barber's Chair when the solid one-piece chair started to come apart. The heaviest part of the chair—the steel base—fell off, landing on Tom's foot and crushing it. Tom fell to the ground while the men ran to lift the heavy base off Tom's foot. After they removed the base, they slowly took off Tom's shoe, and his foot was so gory looking. Tom was screaming in pain. They carried Tom to a car and took him to the Emergency Room.

Tom had to have surgery on his foot and had metal rods placed in his foot to keep everything in the right spot. Tom was on crutches then for a while. It was so horrifying to see those metal rods protruding from his toes, and it looked so painful. The Doctors told Tom that he needed to twist the little metal rods that were protruding from his toe thru out the day every day. That looked so creepy and painful. We spoke with Tom, and it seemed that the house had gotten to attack Tom one last time. It was as if we were being shown that we were never welcome there before and to not come back again.

I don't know why Tom was physically attacked so much. Tom really went through hell in that house with Jami and me. That was the last item to be removed from the house, and to have Tom physically hurt again couldn't have been a random accident. Tom was our protector in that house, and Jami and I felt safe whenever Tom was at our home. The house seemed to want to get even just one last time with Tom, and it did.

18 | THE NEW RENTAL

WE HAD NOW MOVED INTO our next house, which was a rental on the other side of the town. Jami and I were then fifteen and a half years old. That rental we had moved into was such a fresh start. There were no scary feelings when we went up or down the steps in that house. The stairs in the haunted house were so different.

Whenever I walked down the stairs in that haunted house, it seemed like I was walking into an abyss of darkness from which I would not come out of. Jami and Tom felt the same way. The stairs in the new rental were normal. We had lived in a few houses that had stairs, and things were back to normal again.

Tom needed to recover and let his foot heal. That was the last reminder of what we had been through in the other house. We could finally sleep without being scared. Not too long after Tom's foot had healed, he went back to Las Vegas, and we rarely saw him again. We were so fortunate to have Tom there for us throughout our childhood he was such a strength in our life.

I don't know how many months had passed but we were told of a horrible accident that had hurt one of my uncles friends children. The friend was the guy who had sold my uncle the antique Barbers Chair that had crushed Toms foot. The friend had a son who was around ten years old. The little boy was playing outside in the front yard and they lived on a quiet street .A car came down the street and no one knows why his son did what he did. The boy was playing in his front yard and when the car came down the street the boy walked right out of his front yard and into the path of the oncoming car and was hit. The boy lived but was left in a vegative state and had no chance of recovery .No one would ever know why his son walked out in front of that car to be hit. The story of what had happened to that little boy reminded us of the little girl who had rode her bike into the path of Tom on his motorcycle. It was such a tragedy what happened to the little boy.

As time passed a few months later, I met a seventeen-year-old named Phillip. Phillip was tall; he had black hair, brown eyes, and an amazing olive complexion. There was chemistry between us from the first day we looked at each other in class. But there was one problem with Phillip that he didn't know about. I was trading classes in high school with Jami a lot, and Phillip was in Jami's class.

Phillip and I became close, and he soon became my boyfriend after I explained to him that my name was not Jami and that I was Jodi. I wasn't sure how Phillip was going to handle me when I explained that I was an identical twin and that we had changed classes. I had kept my real name from him all that time. He took it pretty good and laughed about it. Phillip and I were together for a year and a half before I told him of what had happened to us in the haunted house.

I was now seventeen years old and had graduated from high school. I was afraid to tell Phillip about the haunted house for numerous reasons. I thought that maybe Phillip would laugh at me and I would be embarrassed for even telling him. To my surprise, Phillip asked if I would show him the house. That house was so terrifying to me even two years later. I was scared to even drive by the old house. I nervously told Phil that I would show him, and we got into his red truck and drove over to the old house.

I told Phillip to stop the car, and I said, "This is it." Gazing at the old house, I looked at the windows and had this scary feeling that something was watching me from the inside. I turned my head away from the house and told Phillip that I didn't want to look at the property. For some reason, I felt that if I had looked any longer at the old house maybe I would see something paranormal staring back at me. I told Phillip that I wanted to leave; we were only there for a few minutes. Those few minutes were too much for me to want to be that close to the old house. Phillip admitted that the house did have a dark look and feeling to it. Being there brought up so many of the scary memories in that house, and I realized how traumatized I was by that property.

We drove back to Phillip's place to watch a movie rental in his room. Phillip was in the bathroom, and I was sitting on the bed, waiting for him to come out to start the movie. Phillip walked slowly into the room and sat at the edge of the bed just facing and staring at the wall. I asked Phillip, "What's wrong?" But he didn't answer. I asked him again two more times, "What's wrong?" Phillip just ignored me and stared motionless at the wall. Finally, I got angry and I raised my voice and said, "Fine, don't answer me." Then Phillip stood up abruptly and slowly walked out of his room. Phillip was wearing black shorts and a white T-shirt with paw print logo tracks on it and Phillip was thin like he normally was; then he walked away.

Phillip walked out through the doorway in that outfit to leave when to my horror Phillip instantly walked in again wearing red sweat pants and sweatshirt that matched. I scooted back to the corner of the bed, terrified of what had just happened. Phillip asked me what was wrong, and I told him what had just occurred. That didn't make sense to me. I wasn't in the old haunted house. "How could that have just happened?" Looking at Phillip, I was terrified at the fact that the ghost Phillip was just as real as the ghosts I had seen in the old house.

That was a solid person as solid as any human being can be. Then I wondered what did that mean as I had just seen Phillip like I had seen Jami and the puppy. Jami hadn't died, so I must have been wrong about her, and I certainly didn't know what that meant by seeing Phillip that way. I was now too scared to be in that bedroom at Phillip's apartment, and I asked him to move into the other bedroom and he did.

A few days passed, and Phillip bought me a beautiful Hummingbird music box. I placed the music box on a shelf in his room. A week later, I was cleaning up Phil's apartment, and I was then on my way to make his bed. As I walked past the shelf with the Hummingbird music box, it flew off the shelf almost hitting me. The music box flew off the shelf, landing four or five feet away, hitting the ground. I stood there and began to get very scared. That music box would have hurt me if I had walked any slower. It was as if something had just thrown the music box at me and barely missed.

The house was silent, and no one was there but me. I was so scared that I was afraid to move out of fear something would hurt me. Finally, as the minutes passed, I decided to make a run for it out of the room and get out of the apartment. I looked at the Hummingbird music box on the ground and saw that a wing had broken off. I felt terrible that Phillip had just bought me that beautiful music box, and it was now broken. I counted till three in my head, and then I ran as fast as I could out of that bedroom and out of the house to my car and drove home to find Jami.

Phillip called me later that evening and asked me if I would like to come over for dinner, and I said sure. My biggest fear was how I was going to explain to Phillip how the beautiful music box had broken. Phillip had an open mind, and he knew that something was wrong when I walked in through the door. I looked at Phillip and told him what had happened to me earlier in the day and how sorry I was that the wing had broken off the Hummingbird. Phillip looked at me with a perplexed look. Phillip told me that as he had picked up the Hummingbird music box to hand to the cashier it had just fallen out of his hands and hit the ground, causing the wing to break off. The store repaired the wing and reattached it for him with ceramic glue.

He tried to make me feel not so bad by telling me, "Jodi, the wing had already broken off the day I bought it, so it wasn't your fault. The piece was already fragile." Phillip walked upstairs with me to get the music box. As we entered the room, I thought, "I hope it's still there and that I didn't just imagine what had happened earlier." We entered Phillip's room, and there it was on the ground—the Hummingbird music box with the broken wing.

Phillip was then concerned that two odd occurrences had happened in his apartment after we had gone to the old haunted house. I wondered if the entity that lived in the house had somehow come back to Phil's house with us. That was a really scary feeling. While Phillip lived in that apartment, nothing else happened, which was a great relief.

Six months later when I turned eighteen, Phillip caught me off guard one day with a question. Phillip came up to me, then bent down on his knee, and opened a ring box. Phillip looked at me and asked me to marry him. I didn't think Phillip had thought about marriage yet since we were still so young. "Yes" was how I answered his proposal. Phillip and I were very happy over the last three years, and I was excited to have Phillip as my husband. When we got married, we moved out of the apartment that Phillip had lived in, which had started to have scary occurrences, and it was a fresh start in a new house.

19 | FOURTEEN YEARS LATER

I WAS NOW AN ADULT and married to Phillip and had children. I had decided to write down what Jami, Tom, and I had gone through in the haunted house when we were young. My daughters were watching me type on the computer about all of the occurrences, and they asked if all of those things had really happened. I told them yes, that those occurrences had really happened. On our next trip to visit Jami in Big Bear, my daughters asked if I would drive them by the old haunted house. I made a very bad decision when I answered my daughters with a yes.

I figured it would be safe to drive quickly past the old house and not stop. Maybe that's what the problem was before with Phillip; when I had shown him the old house, we stopped at the house. This time I wouldn't stop to show my daughters the house; I would point it out as we drove past the old house.

Two things never made sense to me; first was the ghost Jami. I was so happy that we had cheated death. We were thirty-two now, and Jami was alive and we were going to grow old together. Second, Phillip had lived too and not died, so whatever I had seen was wrong. I no longer lived in Big Bear and had moved about seventy miles away. Jami would visit me every two weeks for a couple of days. Jami loved the time she spent with my children. Sadly, she never had children of her own. Jami was just as much a mother to my children as I was. My children called Jami Mami and I was Mom.

The house we lived in at the time was a rental. The house was just a regular three bedroom two bath. We had not lived in the rental very long before odd things started to occur in the house. The occurrences were strikingly similar to the things that Jami and I had witnessed in that house in Big Bear. One day I was walking through the living room, and as I passed a shelf, a small teddy bear flew off the shelf right in back of me. That was exactly what had happened when I was seventeen and the Hummingbird music box flew off the shelf almost hitting me.

I was now not as scared as I had been when I was younger and I was a Christian now. On the ground was the teddy bear and I said out loud, "You jerk, you missed." I picked up the teddy bear and placed it back on the shelf. Having just had that teddy bear being thrown at me, I realized that driving past the old house had reopened a very dangerous situation. I told Phillip of what had happened, and we kept it from the girls, not wanting to scare them.

Phillip and I had to go out of town for the night, and we arranged for two Bible college students to watch the girls for us. Phillip and I returned the next day, and the two young ladies who had watched the girls told us that they needed to talk to us in private before they left. The girls had taken Katie my daughters' bedroom that night, and they were very scared as they told us about something that they had witnessed—something demonic over the night.

The girls were asleep and the young Bible college students were almost asleep too when the TV turned on by itself. They refused to even speak of what they saw on the TV, but what had been the scariest thing was that the TV was unplugged. The Bible college students were very shaken and upset as they tried to explain what they had seen. Then one of the girls said to Phillip and me that they didn't want to go into detail because it was best that we didn't know what they had seen. We tried to get them to tell us what was it that had frightened them so much, but they refused to discuss the subject any further and told us that we needed to have our house blessed.

I remember that it was close to Halloween because something that was unexplainable had happened in the garage. I had bought two dolls that were dressed in Halloween costumes, and they were three feet tall, the same size as a child. I was storing the dolls in the garage till it was time to put them in the front yard. Halloween was getting close and I went into the garage, and there was white doll stuffing on the ground all over my garage. Something had shredded the two dolls to pieces. I looked at the mess all over the ground and I got very nervous. I didn't own anything that was razor sharp and able to shred the dolls like that. Something wanted to make itself known, and I started to become scared.

I wasn't scared for myself, but I was terrified for my children. My daughters came into the garage, and they saw me cleaning up all of the shredded doll pieces and asked me point blank, "What happened to the dolls, Mom?"

I looked at my daughters and just said, "I don't know." I downplayed the situation, not wanting my daughters to realize that something very dangerous had just occurred. I wondered what was it that had shredded the dolls, and that thought alone was scary. Not long after the dolls were shredded, I was given a wonderful opportunity.

I missed my Maltese Frenchy, who had died years earlier, and then a friend said that she needed to find a home for her two-year-old female who had already been named Tootie. It was so exciting to have another dog like my beloved Frenchy again. It was around 5:00 a.m., and I let Tootie out to go to the bathroom. I opened the door that led to the garage; there was another door inside the garage that led to the backyard. There was a very small doggy door attached to the door, which was just big enough for Tootie to fit through.

I was sitting at the table waiting for Tootie to scratch at the door to come back in when I heard her whimper. I opened the door to the garage, but I didn't see Tootie anywhere. Frantically, I started looking around the garage and behind boxes, and there was Tootie lying on the ground. Tootie was bloody and had been shredded throughout her body by something. I screamed for my husband as I picked up Tootie and ran inside carrying her.

My children and my husband came running to the living room asking what had happened. I told them that I had let her out and she had been out only for a few minutes when I heard just one whimper come from the garage and then I found Tootie torn to shreds. I was crying and so were my kids. It didn't make sense how that had just happened. We rushed Tootie to the veterinarian, and they did the best they could to patch her up.

The Veterinarian said that she had been clawed throughout her body by something that had very strong claws and that he wasn't sure what had attacked her. She was not bitten throughout her body like you would expect as if a wild animal had managed to attack her in those few minutes. The veterinarian told us he didn't know if she would make it because her entire body was just so bad; it was the saddest sight looking at her, and she was in so much pain. Tootie survived for a little while, but she ended up dying because of the wounds.

The way Tootie's body was shredded reminded me of what Tom had recently told me about how his cat looked and then had also died. Looking back now, I don't believe that was a coincidence, the same shred marks leading to the same outcome—the loss of a beloved pet. To make matters worse for me, I realized that my dolls were shredded to pieces by something razor sharp and so was Tootie. I shuddered at the thought that something so dangerous was making itself known in our rental house.

20 | THE WEATHER AND JAMI

NOT LONG AFTER TOOTIE WAS attacked, we had our first rainstorm of the season. I thought that it was nice to have some rain since we now lived in the desert and it was so dry most of the year. It started to rain and get windy just like any other storm.

I was inside with my daughters when I noticed the rain was coming up to our sliding glass door. One of my daughters said, "Mom, there's water coming out of the garage." I ran to the garage door and saw that the water in my garage was to my knees. Everything in there was ruined by flood waters. I didn't have a choice but to open my garage and let the water run out otherwise our entire house would have flooded.

I opened the garage just about two feet, enough to let the water run through and get out of the garage. I hadn't expected the force of the water to engulf our belongings and push them out of the garage into the street. I looked at the street, sadly watching precious memories wash down the street that had now become a raging river. There was no way to save our belongings.

Numerous trees were also knocked down on our street and throughout the town. That was very unusual weather for the place where we lived.

I still have not seen that wild kind of rainstorm again. There was one place however where I had seen such an intense rainstorm before—in the haunted Big Bear house. When the rain let up, Jami called me to let me know that she was coming down for a visit. The rain finally stopped, and the roads were then safe to travel on, so I called Jami and told her to come down to visit us.

Jami arrived and we had dinner, and she then spent the evening playing with my daughters and reading books to them.

Everyone was asleep, and it was the middle of the night when I was awoken by yelling. I ran to my daughters' room because that's where it was coming from. I stood at the doorway of my daughters' room and looked straight ahead at the most terrifying sight imaginable.

My daughter was sleeping facing the wall while Jami was holding one of those large, extremely heavy computer monitors in her hands. Jami had the computer monitor literally on her fingertips, holding it over my daughter's head. I screamed, "Oh my *god,* Jami! Stop!" It was then in those seconds, I realized what was happening. Jami was cursing and screaming, and it was as if she was trying to stop herself from smashing my daughter's head in with the computer monitor.

The computer monitor was one of the older, really heavy ones. I could barely lift that heavy monitor, and as I looked at Jami, it was unbelievable that she was holding that monitor over her head with her fingertips as if it weighed nothing.

Instantly Jami looked at me, and I never live a day without thinking of what her face looked like. Jami looked straight at me, and her face was not hers. That face on Jami was distorted and her hazel eyes were then solid black eyes; those similar looking sharp and jagged teeth were the same as I had seen on the figure at the top of the stairs.

Whatever I was witnessing, as I stared at Jami, was supernatural and not my twin sister. Jami's face had structurally changed; it was impossible, yet it was happening right before my eyes. Jami looked at me, and then that face gave way to the most demonic evil grin as it stared at me. I believe that if possession was possible, then I was looking straight at pure evil; that wasn't Jami. The entire chain of events that was unfolding shouldn't have been possible.

I was so scared for my daughter and of what I was looking at. Then instantly Jami's face was normal, and she looked above herself and dropped the computer monitor to the ground. Jami stared at the monitor as she dropped it on the floor, then she looked at my daughter; she knew exactly what she had just almost done. She stared at me looking so confused and just lost. I am positive Jami had no control over herself. Jami had somehow stopped something deep inside herself from fatally injuring my daughter.

At that point, my daughter woke up, and my husband and the rest of the children watched Jami run out of the bedroom. My husband asked me what was going on, and I didn't even know what to say. I went to Jami and asked her what was wrong with her and what was it that had just happened in the room. Jami was so upset and crying that I hugged her and told her that what had almost happened was not her fault.

She told me she had no idea or recollection of what she had almost just done. The thought that she had almost killed her niece was more than she could bear. I told Jami what I had seen and that she was not the one who was in control of that situation. I know what I saw; I am an adult now, and there is more to this life than we know.

Jami left and never slept over again whenever she came to visit us. Jami had no recollection of any of that incident. By all standards, there was no way Jami could have held that huge monitor over her own head with her fingertips like it was a feather. Jami's face should not have been able to change and contort the way it did. After Jami and I talked, she insisted that she had to leave, so she called her boyfriend asking him pick her up around 3:00 a.m. and take her back to her house.

After what happened, we had the Church come and bless our home and all of the walls and doorways with Holy Water. I had not told Jami about having the house blessed. Jami was already really scared about what had happened and I just decided to not discuss with her why I was having my house blessed.

It was a month later, and my daughter was having her birthday party. Jami would then only come to visit for a few hours, then drive back to her home. She made plans to come down for the party and mentioned to me that she didn't feel very good and that she had a headache. I told her that we would all understand if she didn't come down for the birthday party, but Jami insisted that she wouldn't miss her niece's birthday.

Jami pulled into the driveway, and my daughters ran outside to hug her and walk her in. The entry door of our rental house had a collage of pictures that were framed.

The front door had on the back of it a mounted Star of David permanently attached to it. At that point, the house was blessed, and the front door was the main location where the Holy Oil was placed. The Pastor had blessed every corner of the entryway and the door itself after the incident of Jami and the computer monitor. Jami walked in through the front door with my daughters, and she stopped in the entryway and stared straight ahead at the collage of photos.

Jami was just gazing at the wall while my daughters were all standing around her. The girls were so excited to see Jami. That was then when things took an unbelievable change. Out of nowhere, Jami started stomping her feet and spinning in circles so fast and out of control that my daughters screamed and backed up. It was the most intense thing I had witnessed, and that time it was in front of Phillip, my children, and other adults. Everyone just panicked and froze, watching her stomp her feet and spin herself in circles. It was something that was so visually terrifying.

Jami suddenly collapsed onto the ground and had a massive seizure. Phillip ran to Jami to hold her during the seizure and make sure that she didn't swallow her tongue. I ran for the phone and called 911. Everyone else who was witnessing that was stricken with fear as they watched Phillip holding her. I spoke to the operator and started crying and begging for them to send help. I was afraid Jami was going to die. The seizure that Jami was having was lasting too long. The seizure just wouldn't stop. Finally, Jami went limp in Phillip's arms and stopped convulsing.

Jami started to wake up and come through to wonder why she was on the ground in Phillip's arms and why was everyone staring at her. I rushed to Jami's side, and Jami whispered to me, "Help me. Please help me." I asked her what was it that she needed help with, and she asked me to help her get to one of the bedrooms to lie down. I told her that an ambulance was on the way, and she got upset and said that she was fine and that she just needed to lie down. I walked Jami to my daughter's bed and then Jami asked me what had happened.

I told Jami, "I don't really know what just happened, but you had a massive seizure."

The ambulance showed up and took Jami to the hospital, where she stayed for a few days till she was stable. When the ambulance took Jami, I asked everyone to leave the party with their traumatized and scared children. When everyone was gone, Phillip and I discussed what we had just witnessed. Jami had no idea that we had the house blessed and that the focal point was the front door.

Phillip and I both agreed on what we had seen. I don't think that I believe in demons being able to take over a person's body. But what we saw sure looked just like that. It looked as if Jami was possessed by something that couldn't get through our front entryway. When whatever it was inside of Jami couldn't get past the walls, it appeared as if something demonic in nature threw a fit. There was a line it seemed that Jami couldn't cross, and Jami had no idea that we had that area heavily blessed.

I was so scared for Jami; something was so very wrong. I bought Jami a pink Bible and gave it to her. A Bible was all that I could think of that could help her. When Jami was released from the hospital, she came back to my house. I was planning on her staying for a while so I could watch over her and take care of her. Before Jami was released, the Doctor had taken me aside in the hospital and talked to me about Jami.

I was told that Jami was very weak and in the end stages of alcoholism and that she was going to die if she didn't stop drinking. I didn't even know that she had a drinking problem. Jami had kept that a secret from me, and I had no idea that she was sick. Jami had lost a lot of weight, but I didn't realize truly how thin she was. When we arrived at my house, Jami told me her ride was on its way to take her back to her house. I told her that she couldn't leave, and we got into an argument. Jami became furious and told me, "Jodi, I am not safe to have in your house. I am leaving, and nothing you can say will make me stay here. I am a danger to the girls and my mind is made up." In that instant as I looked at Jami I had to agree with her decision. Jami was right; if I made her stay, she really could hurt someone.

Neither one of us knew what was happening to Jami physically, but we both knew she had no control over some of her actions. Jami loved my daughters so much that she refused the only person who could help her, which was me. Half an hour later, Jami's boyfriend showed up to take her home. I looked at Jami and begged her to stop drinking and to stay on her seizure medication when she left. The Doctor was so sure that she was at such a dangerous point with regards her body; then she just left. I was so worried about Jami; something was very wrong. As Jami drove away, I had this horrible overwhelming feeling of sadness.

21 | JAMI'S CHANGING

THE NEXT DAY I CALLED Jami to check on her, and again I told her what the Doctor had told me about her frail condition. We were then thirty-two, and as I sit back and think about it, Jami's clothing style had changed. She started wearing baggy layers of clothes. I just figured she felt comfortable in those outfits or was dressing warm since she lived in the mountains. I made a phone call to Jami and pleaded her, "Stop, just stop drinking." I told her that I didn't want her to die and that she needed to listen to the Doctor.

Jami told me that she would stop drinking and that she would be fine. I soon found out that she had already begun drinking the night she returned home.

I could hear it now in Jami's voice; as we spoke, I realized she wasn't sober. The Doctor was very firm with me about how bad off she was. If Jami started to drink again, she was at risk of dying from back-to-back seizures and would not ever wake up. The Doctor said that she was in the most danger of dying on day four of detoxing. I guess that's the mark that many severe alcoholics don't survive if they go cold turkey. Jami didn't believe that she was that bad, but I did.

I told Jami to take her seizure meds and that I would call her all day long for the next four days. Jami refused to detox in my home, and she didn't want me to witness her detoxing. So day one, I called Jami all day long checking in on her, and she was doing fine. Day two came along, and again I called Jami all day long, checking in on her. On the third day, Jami said her body was hurting and she had found herself on the ground. I told Jami that she must be having seizures and the body pain was probably from hitting the ground. Jami told me that she didn't think that she was having seizures because her boyfriend was watching her round the clock and he would have told her if she was having seizures. I told Jami that I was worried about her. The next day that was day four was fast approaching. Jami assured me that she would be fine and she said, "Jodi, I've made it through the last three days and I am fine. I will make it through day four, don't worry." Then I told her goodnight that night and that `I would talk to her in the morning.

I was making breakfast for my daughter when the phone rang around 8:00 a.m. The minute I picked up the phone and heard the voice of Jami's boyfriend I knew she had died. I started screaming into the phone at her boyfriend, "What happened? What did you do?" Jami's boyfriend told me he had gone to the store and had been gone only thirty minutes, and when he returned, he found Jami on the ground in their bedroom. He told me that he tried CPR and called 911, but it was too late, and she was declared dead. I told her boyfriend, "Don't you let the coroner take her. I will be there in forty-five minutes, and you had better stall them!"

I called Phillip and pulled my daughters out of school, and we drove to Jami's house. I saw the ambulance in the driveway as we pulled in. I had been crying the entire car ride, in shock that she was dead. I couldn't believe she was dead. I needed to see her.

I ran through Jami's house to her bedroom, and there she was on the ground as if she was just asleep. I collapsed onto the ground and cradled Jami in my arms; she was so thin I could feel her rib cage. I stroked her hair, and I was crying so hard, telling Jami, "Wake up, please wake up." But she was just lifeless. I stayed in the bedroom till the coroner made me leave and put Jami down. I was walking out of Jami's room when I looked in her bathroom and saw that she had bought blonde hair dye and that it was already mixed and just needed to be applied to her hair. I immediately thought back to the time when I was a kid and had seen Jami. The apparition Jami had blonde hair, the same color as the one that she had on the counter. Jami's hair was the longest that it had ever been in her life. Jami was also so skinny; she weighed seventy-eight pounds when she died. The only thing that didn't make sense was the peach-colored dress. I was now in shock that I had lost my beloved twin, Jami, and I was the one who had the responsibility of arranging her funeral. I had reached my breaking point, so I called my big brothers and asked them to help me with the funeral, and they stepped up and helped me through the toughest day I had ever had to endure.

I arranged for our Pastor and some Bible college students to do Jami's funeral. Phillip and I went into the church to meet with the Pastor and to discuss what we wanted to be said about Jami. When the Pastor asked me the first question, I started to respond, but the minute I opened my mouth to speak, I couldn't. I could only cry and wasn't able to speak. Phillip looked at me and hugged me, then he asked me if I would like him to answer the questions. I could only nod my head to indicate that I agreed. That was such a horrible feeling trying to talk and then not being able to do so.

When it was time to plan Jami's funeral, we were told to buy a dress that was at least knee length and loose fitting. When I was told that, I became nervous about having to buy her that dress and hoped that it wouldn't be peach colored. My husband knew that story from me and Jami through all these years about a dress that was peach colored and that Jami would die in it. What didn't make sense before was that Jami didn't die in that dress or any dress for that matter.

Phillip and I went to many stores, trying to find a proper dress, and we just couldn't find the right dress. There was one more store to go, and I just couldn't handle the day any longer. My husband looked through the door inside the clothing store and turned white and froze. He looked at me and said "Jodi, stay here. I don't want you to see this. I see it, the dress from here. It's exactly as you said it would be." I sat on the ground outside the store, holding my head and sobbing as my husband purchased the dress.

The clerk told my husband that the dress had just been returned that morning and put on the shelf minutes before he bought it. When Phillip was walking me to the car, he looked at me and said, "Oh my god, I am next. I am going to die. How long do I have, Jodi?" he asked.

I looked at Phillip and said, "I don't know anything or if you will die. This whole thing, the way Jami died, was right but wrong from what I saw in that house in Big Bear." I told Phillip that maybe he wasn't going to die; maybe he would be hurt badly at some point. I was trying to be optimistic at that point.

We took the dress to the funeral director, and then he told me that we needed to purchase some socks too. I lost it and said, "I can't do this." I had someone else go buy the socks for Jami. The socks that the person bought for Jami turned out to be bootie socks just like the exact kind I had seen her wear with that dress twenty years earlier. The person that bought the socks could have bought any kind of style, but of course it had to be the same style I had seen on the Jami apparition.

All of that was too overwhelming to me. I went home and took a nap and had a bizarre dream. I was dreaming that I was looking at a photo of me and Jami, and then the picture started to rip apart and Jami's side fell to the ground; mine was still in my hand. I woke up in a panic and realized that it was no longer the two of us; I was alone now and by myself. Phillip was such a strength for me. I could barely talk; all I could do was cry.

The day of Jami's funeral our dear friend Ronda had shown up and I looked at her and told her to stay calm when she looked at Jami in the open casket. Ronda knew of the story and the peach colored dress from when we were teenagers. I was an absolute emotional mess on that day. Burying Jami had been the hardest thing that I had ever had to do. During the funeral our friend from High School and her father had walked in to pay there respects .I remember that Jami had mentioned that she loved the Bag Pipes and my friends father knew how to play them. The sound of Amazing Grace being played with Bag Pipes was the most sad yet beautiful music I had ever heard.

22 | A YEAR AND A HALF LATER

I DON'T KNOW WHY I saw Jami in the way that I did. Watching the events unfold from her long blonde hair to being very thin and the exact dress she was buried in was overwhelming. We tried to cheat death, but I realize now that I couldn't. That house has something seriously wrong with it; maybe the property in the area is tainted by something. It seemed that there was a very powerful vicious unseen force.

I've said over the years that there's no amount of money that could get me to go back inside that house. I was young when I went through all of that. I am now forty-one, and honestly I couldn't handle seeing anything like that again. I often wonder what the new tenants have gone through, if anything at all. Not a day goes by that I don't think about that house and Jami. You can't cheat death is what I've learned. We should also love those around us because one day they wont be here anymore and death is permanent.

If I could do just one thing over, it would be to keep Jami with me and not let her detox without me. I would have saved her and never left her alone. Seeing what I saw in that house didn't do any good to save Jami. If anything, it was a cruel evil thing to show me. Seeing the ghost Jami did not mean that I could save her; it was meant to torment me every day till she died. Every day I worried about Jami dying in that peach-colored dress. How cruel it was that Jami and I both worried all of those years about her imminent death, and the irony was that she would be Dead in and not Die in that dress. Whatever is in that house I hope someday it gets paid back for what it did to all of us. I hope there is justice on the other side.

What should have been the end of the story with Jami passing away unfortunately was not the end of that nightmare. As I was writing this chapter, my phone rang, but I didn't answer; then the phone rang again, so I answered it. A female on the other line asked, "Is this Jodi?"

I said, "Yes."

The female voice said, "Hello, I am Jami, and I am with—" And I hung up the phone.

So what was that about just now! I don't believe it was a coincidence just now. I know that logically it was just a telemarketer calling, but the timing and the name were so emotionally cruel.

Sorry for the subject change; I wasn't anticipating that happening or leaving it in the book, but I've decided to leave that in here as a reminder to me that odd things are still happening, and that was definitely odd. So back to a year and a half after Jami had died. I was coming out of the shock I had been in for a while.

Phillip, our children, and I were going to go visit his father and have dinner with him. We had been having Sunday night dinners with my father-in-law ever since I was fifteen. We drove to my father-in-law's and had a wonderful visit and a nice dinner with him and the children. It was time to go home, and we all gave my father-in-law a good-bye hug and said that we would see him next week. We all got into our SUV; I was the driver.

We were driving home on the highway, and out of nowhere Phillip yelled, "Oh my god, Jodi, stop!" I looked in Phillip's direction, and as my feet pressed down on the brakes, I saw why I needed to stop. There was an access road to enter the four-lane highway that went in both directions. There was a stop sign at the access road.

I screamed, "Girls, hold on tight." Then in slow motion there was this car that drove through the stop sign and stopped right in front of our SUV. We were driving approximately 65–70 mph and there was not enough time to stop; we were going to hit that car. I saw the person's face as we collided, and she had a blank expression on her face. Then my airbag deployed, and I heard the noise of metals as our vehicles collided, making that awful screeching noise.

I woke up right after the impact and asked if everyone was OK. I looked in the back and saw that my daughters in the back were alive, then I looked at myself and I was covered in blood. I didn't feel anything but adrenalin, and I didn't know why I was covered in blood. Sitting next to me was my daughter and the blood was hers. She was moaning that her back was broken, and her teeth and face had so much blood on them. Then Phillip started to move but yelled out in pain.

Phillip was in very bad condition like my daughter. The car started to smoke and catch fire. I had my daughters in the back run to the side of the highway while I carried Sara out of the car. I couldn't wait for the paramedics to remove her; we didn't have that much of time. I went back for Phil. He was trapped in the vehicle, and I couldn't get him out; he was dying. That was the worst situation I could have ever been in.

While my daughters sat on the side of the highway, I ran back to Phillip and tried again to get him out. This time I realized why Phillip was trapped. Phillip's leg had broken in the form of a Z. That was the most horrifying sight to see. I didn't know a leg could even look like that, and his leg was trapping him in the car.

I told Phillip, "I am not letting you die alone. I am staying with you." Phillip was getting weak, and then he saw that our daughter Brittney had wandered down the highway in a daze. Brittney, our six-year-old, was walking into the oncoming traffic. My other daughter, Brea, was holding Sara and pinching her and slapping her face to keep her awake. There was no one to get Brittney.

Phillip in his last words said, "I love you, Jodi, but you can't stay with me. You have to save Brittney. Now go." I kissed and hugged Phillip and told him "I love you so much!" I knew he was right .If I did not save Brittney she was going to be killed by oncoming traffic.

I was crying, and I was so angry and mad that all of this was so out of control. I realized how alone I was. I limped down the highway to get Brittney who was in shock. I returned to Brea and Sara, and we all sat together, then Brea said, "We have to get Dad."

I looked at Brea and said, "Dad's trapped. We can't get him out."

Brea got quite upset, and she said, "Hold Sara. I am not leaving him in there." I held Sara as Brea ran to Phillip. Brea was there with Phillip for a few seconds, and then I saw her come running back to me, crying. Brea now knew what I had said about Phillip being trapped in the burning SUV. There was nothing any of us could do; we felt so hopeless.

As I sat there, I told the girls we all needed to turn away from the SUV. I didn't want the girls to see their dad burn alive. We turned away from the SUV; all of us were crying. That moment when there was no way for Phillip to survive, I sat with my daughters and prayed for a miracle to happen. We prayed to *God*, begging that somehow he would let Phillip survive.

The minute I said "Amen" an off duty fireman came running with a fire extinguisher and put the fire out. He was followed by off duty paramedics and an off duty nurse, then I heard above us a medevac helicopter, which landed behind us. It was truly a miracle; it was as if the cavalry had been called in. We suffered many injuries, but Phillip and my daughter Sara had the life-threatening ones. I sat there as they worked on getting Phillip out of the car, and I thought, "This isn't right. This isn't how I saw Phillip." I actually took comfort in that. I knew that he wasn't going to die right there at least. I thought of Jami and how badly I needed her there then and how insane all of that was.

My daughters and I were put in one ambulance while Phillip was put in a different one. Another of life's cruel turn of events was happening. They took me and the children to a different hospital than Phillip. When we arrived at the Emergency Room, I kept asking whether my husband was alive, but no one knew. I called the Pastor at my church and asked for help. I explained that Phillip was alone at the other hospital and that I needed someone to be with him and to let me know how he was. Phillip told me later that he refused to let the Doctors work on him till he had spoken to me to see if everyone had lived. I didn't know at that time, but Phillip was dying from his internal injuries. The Doctor needed to set Phillips leg fully awake and get him into surgery. Phillip was going into shock. The Doctors gave into Phillip's demand, and so a nurse walked into the Emergency Room and told me that my husband was on the phone.

Phillip was alive; he said he was in bad condition and didn't know how bad he was. One Pastor had just shown up to be with Phillip and another Pastor had shown up with me and the children. I told Phillip that I loved him and that we were all going to live although there were serious injuries. Then they made Phillip hang up. I didn't know if Phillip was still going to live or not, but I took comfort in knowing that at least Phillip was not alone if he did die.

Then things got worse for me. The Doctor told me that Sara needed to be transported to a children's hospital to be treated. I needed to stay with Sara, but then all of us were about to be split up. The Doctors released my two daughters Brea and Brittney. The Pastors took them home for me to Katie, my eldest daughter, who had stayed home to watch our one-year-old Grace. Fortunately, Grace and Katie had stayed home for that trip to visit their grandpa. They had not come down for that visit because Grace was sick.

My mind was in a whirlwind. I had Phillip at one hospital, and now I had to go with Sara to a children's hospital an hour away while my injured daughters were at home with my eldest daughter watching them. I was emotionally spread thin and worried about everyone. I am so thankful to my church for what they did for us. The Church rallied together, and one of the Pastors' wife stayed with the children at home, so I knew they were OK. The ladies group made sure that the children had hot meals each night and plenty of food in the fridge. Our dear friends from the church kept checking on the children and Phillip for me. I had thought I was so alone, but the generosity of so many friends and strangers came to our aid; it was such a humbling grateful feeling.

Three days later, Sara was released to go home, but she required additional surgery. I took Sara in her wheelchair to the hospital to see

Phillip who was in intensive care. That was the first time I was able to see Phillip since they had taken us away in the hospital. Phillip looked so hurt and Sara looked just as bad. We all hugged and cried as we were so grateful that our family lived. Phillip was released seven days later.

When I had everyone home, we all looked like we had been in a huge battle. We were all so bruised up and hurt, more so Phillip and Sara with their injuries. Phillip was going to require many more surgeries over the next few months to repair injuries in his body. The Doctors needed to wait for Phillip to regain some strength first before doing any further surgery. Over the next two months, Phillip's weight dropped dramatically; he was thinner than he had been in high school. When I noticed the weight loss, I started to become worried.

Phillip was bedridden now, and he required more T-shirts, so I placed an online order for five T-shirts in every color but white. Phillip never wore a white T-shirt after I saw the ghost of him in his apartment wearing one. We were all superstitious about white T-shirts now, including our daughters. A week later, Phillip's T-shirts showed up, and all of my daughters were there when I opened the box. As I opened the box and pulled out the shirts from inside, my eldest daughter Kate gasped, and I did too. Kate scolded me for ordering an entire box of white t-shirts. I was stunned as I looked at the box.

The order form receipt was inside, and I knew I hadn't made that kind of mistake. I pulled out the receipt, and there it was—not one white shirt had been ordered and the colors were wrongly picked. I showed the receipt to my daughter, and then Phillip wheeled himself to the doorway to see what all the commotion was about in the living room. Phillip looked at my hands and on the table, and he saw all of the white T-shirts. His face became pale. Then Phillip became angry, and he said, "Give me those T-shirts. I am not afraid to wear them and I am not going to die." So we kept the T-shirts. Phillip to this day insists on white ones too because he says he's not going to be dictated on how he lives his life over something that happened a long time ago.

The time had come for Phillip's surgery. They dressed him in his surgical attire and then allowed me to see him before they started working on him. I walked over to Phillip and hugged him, and as I leaned in to hug Phillip, I saw that there was a paw print logo on the chest of his surgical gown just like I had seen on the ghost Phillip's white T-shirt when I was young.

I started to have all of these thoughts in my head like, "Do I tell Phillip what I am seeing or not? Do I tell him to fight like hell in the surgery?" I didn't know what to say.

I was looking at Phillip, and he asked me, "Jodi, what's wrong?"

I looked at Phillip and said, "I want you to stay calm, and I don't know if I should tell you this, but I am going to. Phillip, look down under your chin by your chest."

Phillip looked worried, and as he looked at the paw logo, he freaked out, saying, "I'm going to die in this surgery, aren't I?" I told Phil that I didn't know but that I would be right there waiting for him when he came out of the surgery.

I told Phillip, "Fight like hell in there. Don't you leave me and the girls." And then they took Phillip away.

What I hadn't told Phillip was that the garment bag holding his belongings had paw prints on it; the socks they had on him had paw prints too. It was too much to handle. It seemed like it couldn't be happening, and I had no control over what was going on in the surgery room.

A few hours later, they let me know that the surgery was a success and that he was on his way to his hospital bed. Phillip was very groggy from the anesthesia; the nurse had just checked his vitals, and he was normal. The surgery had gone fine. I was so relieved. The nurse told me that she would be back in an hour to check on Phillip. Since Phillip was stable, I told Phillip and the nurse that I was going to go over to the vending machine to get a drink with a lot of caffeine and that I would be right back.

I was gone maybe only two minutes. When I walked back into Phillip's room, he was sitting upright; he was looking gray and shaking. He couldn't talk. I ran to Phil and felt that he was burning up. I paged the nurse that it was an emergency and that Phillip was in shock. I started yelling at Phillip, "Stay with me. The nurse is coming." They started medications on Phillip. They told me that they were not sure whether he was going to survive the night or not; it was fifty–fifty.

I kept giving ice water to Phillip all night, and I kept him cool with a washcloth and laid on his bed, holding him. I just couldn't lose Phillip too. I watched him like a hawk all night, and I prayed over him and begged *God* to let him stay longer with us. Then morning came, and I felt Phillip move; he slowly opened his eyes to gaze at me, looking so tired; he had survived!

He is now seriously disabled and in immense pain twenty-four hours a day from the bodily injury due to the crash and is bedridden for the majority of the day now. He has lost his health but not his spirit. How Phillip makes it through each day in so much pain and always undergoing more surgeries is amazing to me. I am so grateful that Phillip is alive. My heart breaks as I watch Phillip with his daily struggles. I don't know if we cheated death or not. But the things that happened were eerily similar to the Phillip I had seen in his apartment—the way Phillip would be very thin, the white T-shirt, the paw print logo, and him not being able to speak, just sitting upright.

As I sit here reviewing my writing, I think about Tom and the motorcycle crash that he was in at the old house in Big Bear. Interestingly, when I spoke with Tom on the phone about that crash I realized that there were some very real similarities. Tom was riding the motorcycle, and the girl drove right in front of the motorcycle and stopped. Tom realized what she had done as he got close to her; he said her face was so blank and emotionless and her injury was to her leg. The person responsible for our crash had only injured her leg too. Also in our crash, the person's facial expression was the same. She rolled right through the stop sign to just stop directly in front of our SUV. Her face was blank like she didn't even realize what she was doing. Later we were told that she had no memory of even getting in the car or driving before the crash. It seems similar to me, but that's just my thoughts about both crashes.

THREE YEARS LATER

I HAVE FINALLY FINISHED THE book that I had started so long ago. There seemed to be a struggle to finish it for a while. I drove to Big Bear by myself to face my fears with that house and to go to the old graveyard and apologize once again for the childhood stupidity. I am not scared of that house any longer. I am too angry at that house to be scared.

I drove to the old house and looked at it. The house had not changed at all over all those years. I stepped out of the car and quietly said to the house, "I hate you and whatever exists inside." I got back in the car and drove home. Well, that wasn't a good idea. I may not be scared any longer, but what was in that house is still there. I am positive.

The week I returned home from Big Bear, it was dusk out and I heard a lot of noise outside. I walked to the front door and looked above me toward the sky. There were maybe two hundred black crows all hovering in a circle above our home. There were so many that you could hardly see the sky. All of our neighbors witnessed that as I yelled for Phillip and my children to come outside to see the crows. We all stood there silently looking at that ominous oddity of nature that was occurring on our property. When it became completely dark, most of the crows went away.

Three crows seemed to stay, and they now live in my trees and occasionally make that horrible crowing sound. I don't know what that was supposed to mean having so many crows circling our property, but it was odd. There are more occurrences that happened after the crows, but I shall end my book here. I am not ready to go into further details; I don't think I ever will.

The rest of the story shall stay in my family. I have a lot of theories about all of that, and I am keeping them to myself, but to you the reader, maybe all of this will make some form of sense to you. One final note—my beliefs from enduring such bizarre occurrences have made me a firm believer in haunted houses and unseen demonic entities. In my circumstances, the only time I felt safe in those scary times was in my faith. If evil demonic entities exist, then surely a miraculous *God* exists.

In Loving Memory of Jami Lee Pizinger
Born June 29, 1970
Entered into Rest August 25, 2004
My Beloved Twin Sister and Aunt "Mamie" to My Children